# HOW DO WE KNOW?

*TO* my great friend, Clarence

*. . . one who seeks truth*
*and thus attains freedom*

all my best!

*[signature]*

LEONARD E. READ

# HOW DO WE KNOW?

The Foundation for Economic Education, Inc.
Irvington-on-Hudson, New York 10533
1981

THE AUTHOR AND PUBLISHER

Leonard E. Read has been president of The Foundation for Economic Education since it was organized in 1946.

The Foundation is a nonpolitical, nonprofit, educational institution. Its senior staff and numerous writers are students as well as
teachers of the free market, private ownership, limited government
rationale. Sample copies of the Foundation's monthly study journal, *The Freeman,* are available on request.

Published October 1981

ISBN-0-910614-68-7

# CONTENTS

# 1

# HOW DO WE KNOW?

*He who calls in the aid of an equal
understanding, doubles his view; and
he who profits of a superior understanding, raises his powers to a level
with the height of the superior understanding he unites with.*
                    **—EDMUND BURKE**

Edmund Burke (1729–97) here gives me reason enough for so
frequently calling to my aid this great statesman and source of
wisdom. He expertly counsels how understanding—knowledge—
can be achieved.

All wish to possess knowledge, but few, comparatively speaking, are willing to pay the price.                    —*Juvenal*

In my view, this Roman poet (60–140), over-assessed the citizens of Italy. Never in Italy or any other country, during the last
twenty centuries, has *everyone* wished to possess knowledge. To

1

many millions, ignorance is bliss; they are happy in their doldrums—"low spirits."

However, this poet was absolutely right in asserting that few are willing to pay the price for knowledge. The price?

> Real knowledge, like everything else of value, is not to be attained easily. It must be worked for, studied for, thought for, and more than all, must be prayed for.     —*Thomas Arnold*

If an individual fails to work for an ever-increasing understanding of ideas not yet known, he or she lapses into a stalemate—that is, a no-improvement—category. Asleep at the switch, as we say!

> All growth depends on activity. There is no development physically or intellectually without effort, and effort means *work*. Work is not a curse; it is the prerogative of intelligence, the only means to manhood, and the measure of civilization.
>
> —*Calvin Coolidge*

Everyone who pursues an improved understanding of how freedom works its wonders makes a contribution to a higher-grade civilization. More people than now must make freedom their lifelong study.

> The man who has acquired the habit of study, though for only one hour every day in the year, and keeps to the one thing studied till it is mastered, will be startled to see the progress he has made at the end of a twelvemonth.
>
> —*Edward Bulwer-Lytton*

Among the thousands of freedom devotees known to me, I am unaware of a single one who has *mastered* Creation at the human level, and it is my view that no mortal being ever will. Otherwise, this English novelist's observation confirms my own, namely, the enormous advancement in an improved understanding of liberty made possible by daily study. These individuals attain an attractive status. Others seek their tutorship. This is the only way learning is advanced!

The English educator, Thomas Arnold (1795–1842), tells us that knowledge must be "worked for," and "thought for." And there is another "*must,*" namely, knowledge "must be prayed for."

> Prayer is not eloquence, but earnestness; not the definition of helplessness, but the feeling of it; not figures of speech, but earnestness of soul.     *—Hannah More*

"Eloquence" has two meanings: (1) the favorable kind: "articulate, fluent, smooth-spoken" and (2) "passionate, glib, silver-tongued, weak." The English author, More, used "eloquence" in the derogatory sense, that is, as the opposite of "earnestness."

Those who are truly earnest in the pursuit of freedom more often than not find the means to such a glorious end. If not, they create their own means, and they succeed in their explanations.

> Is not prayer a study of truth, a sally of the soul into the unfound infinite? No man ever prayed heartily without learning something.     *—Emerson*

The Sage of Concord stresses the word "heartily," meaning "from the whole heart." This is to be distinguished from prayers "repeated by rote"—the copycat variety—imitation. Let us every day of every year say our prayers for a return to freedom, and *heartily.*

I am often criticized—in a friendly way—for so copiously quoting those whose wisdom is far superior to mine, Edmund Burke, for instance. "Why don't you confine yourself to your own thinking?" My reason? Most individuals do not have available to them such resources as are available to us at FEE. So why not share the wisdom of seers—those who have seen what most of us have not—with freedom aspirants!

Now to "How Do We Know?" that is, become more knowledgeable? Unquestionably, the first step is to become sharply aware of how little we know. The know-it-all is a know-nothing! The more we practice what we know, the more shall we know what to practice. If we have an awareness of how freedom works its miracles, we will, without question, become a freedom practitioner!

The above is consistent with Burke's excellent knowledge, "He who calls in the aid of an equal understanding, doubles his view."

In many things, it is not well to say, "know thyself"; it is better to say, "know others."                      —*Menander*

How to double our knowledge? Share and share alike!

To comprehend a man's life it is necessary to know not merely what he does, but also what he purposely leaves undone. There is a limit to the work that can be got out of a human body or a human brain, and he is a wise man who wastes no energy on pursuits for which he is not fitted; and he is still wiser who, from among the things that he can do well, chooses and resolutely follows the best.                      —*Gladstone*

Reflect on the countless pursuits for which each of us is "not fitted." I, for instance, have no competence as an astronomer, a singer or composer of music, these three being among thousands of my incompetencies. Different people fall into different categories; some excel in several things, but no one excels in everything. Briefly, what any one person knows, compared to all knowledge, is infinitesimal. What we are ignorant of is beyond our powers of imagination! However, there are a goodly number of men and women whose highest aspiration is an improved understanding and explanation of freedom. Let us resolutely follow our best!

Wrote the author of a remarkable book, *Human Destiny*, Lecomte du Noüy: "To really participate in the Divine Task, man must place his ideals as high as possible, out of reach if necessary." Liberty for one and all is, indeed, one of mankind's highest ideals. Out of reach? No one does or ever has perfectly understood its miraculous potentialities. What to do? Study and discover the answer to this question: *how do we know?*

# 2

# READ GOOD BOOKS FOR IMPROVED THINKING

*To use books rightly, is to go to them for help; to appeal to them when our own knowledge and power fail; to be led by them into wider sight and purer conception than our own, and to receive from them the united sentence of the judges and councils of all time, against our solitary and unstable opinions.* **—JOHN RUSKIN**

This English critic, essayist and social reformer (1819–1900), in one of his books, gave posterity this council: "A speaker should inform his audience, at the very outset, where he stands."

I have heeded this admonition in several hundred lectures delivered during the past 24 years. I explain that I like all kinds of weather—hot or cold, rain, sleet, snow, hail, fog, or whatever. This is my way of expressing appreciation that God, not the government, is in charge. My audiences know, at the very outset, that I espouse the freedom way of life and dislike politicians trying to run our lives. *The reading of a good book improved my thinking!*

6

Here is an outstanding example having to do with the value of good books. Leo Tolstoy (1828–1910) was, according to *The Columbia Encyclopedia,* a "Russian philosopher and novelist, one of the world's greatest writers." In his book, *The Law of Love and The Law of Violence,* he wrote: "From the day when the first members of councils placed exterior authority higher than interior, that is to say, recognized the decisions of men united in councils as more important and more sacred than reason and conscience: on that day began lies that caused the loss of millions of human beings and which continue their unhappy work to the present day."

At the very moment I began this essay, a university professor from Wisconsin came to my desk and asked where he could find this example of Tolstoy's wisdom. Having used this truth many times in my own books, I pointed to it in *The Free Man's Almanac.* A good book of the last century was one source of a book of mine in 1974. I suspect that the professor, a great writer and freedom devotee, might include this in his next book. Observe how those of us looking for moral and politico-economic help go to books, hoping they are good. The good ones capture the wisdom of sages—present and past.

By the way, a chapter in my book, *Awake for Freedom's Sake,* is entitled "War and Peace," the title of a two-volume creation of Tolstoy's. He and yours truly see eye-to-eye on this subject.

Let us not be misled that the mere reading of books will improve our thinking. Many are bad and intellectually demoralizing. Wrote the English author, John Murray (1851–1928): "A dose of poison can do its work only once, but a bad book can go on poisoning people's minds for any length of time."

As to length of time, Plato, the Greek philosopher of about 24 centuries ago, advanced the philosopher-king idea. Abbreviated, he said that everyone—no exception—". . . should get up, or

move, or wash, or take his meals . . . only if he has been told to
do so. In a word, he should teach his soul, by long habit, never to
dream of acting independently and to become utterly incapable of
it.''

The same idea is to be found in a book published in 1935, *Man
the Unknown,* by the distinguished scientist, Dr. Alexis Carrel.
Most of the book is devoted to skillful and critical analysis of our
decline into the planned economy and the welfare state—socialism. After enumerating ever so many advanced specializations, he
observes that no one possesses all knowledge. Of course no one
does, but Dr. Carrel believes a few *could* and *should* possess it all.
Reflect on his solution:

> In about twenty-five years of uninterrupted study, one could
> learn these sciences. At the age of fifty, those who have submit-
> ted themselves to this discipline could effectively *direct* the
> construction of the human being and of a civilization. . . .
>
> We have to *intervene* in the fundamental organic and mental
> processes. These processes are man himself. But man has no
> independent existence. He is bound to his environment. In order
> to *remake* him, we have to transform his world. . . .
>
> A group, although very small, is capable of eluding the harm-
> ful influence of the society of its epoch by *imposing* upon its
> members rules of conduct modeled on *military* or monastic
> discipline. . . .
>
> Such a minority would be in a position to impose by persua-
> sion or perhaps *by force,* other ways of life upon the major-
> ity. . . .
>
> We must single out the children who are endowed with high
> potentialities, and develop them as completely as possi-
> ble. . . .

Who are "we"? It's a million-to-one bet that "we" would

never have singled out that 12-year-old newsboy in Michigan, Thomas Alva Edison.

This is precisely the kind of moral politico-economic nonsense that is bedeviling our society today. The lesson this has to teach? Wisely choose the books we read!

The English essayist, Joseph Addison (1672–1719) had an excellent thought about good books: "Books create legacies that genius leaves mankind, to be delivered down from generation to generation, as presents to those that are yet unborn."

Great books bring to us and our progeny the wisdom, the enlightenment, and the common sense of the profoundest thinkers of all time. A late friend of mind, Dr. Thomas Nixon Carver, Professor of Political Economy, Harvard University, gave me his judgment that "The two most important books ever written were Adam Smith's *Wealth of Nations* and the Holy Bible." What a boon to mankind they have been, especially in the formation of our own nation.

Let me conclude with a brilliant observation by the American divine, Henry Giles (1809–82): "The silent influence of books, is a mighty power in the world; and there is a joy in reading them with desire and enthusiasm—Silent, passive and noiseless though they may be, they yet set in action countless multitudes, and change the order of nations."

And change the order of nations? How about the U.S.A.? *Wealth of Nations* had an enormous influence on our Founding Fathers. And the Holy Bible? It was responsible for overthrowing government as the endower of men's rights and placing the Creator there! Result? For at least twelve decades, the freest nation that ever existed: *Liberty for one and all!*

# 3

# THE OPPONENT OF HAPPINESS

*I have never been able to conceive
how any rational being could pro-
pose happiness to himself from the
exercise of power over others.*
**—THOMAS JEFFERSON**

Reflect on what a great American was Jefferson (1743–1826). My
Encyclopedia gives his record:

> Third president of the United States (1801–1809). A gentleman
> and a scholar of thorough legal and diplomatic training. Drafted
> the Declaration of Independence, became governor of Virginia
> (1779–1781), was U.S. minister to France (1785–1789), and
> founded the Democratic-Republican party as whose candidate
> he won the presidential election and became the successor of
> John Adams. As an opponent of the federative party he was
> bitterly opposed to Alexander Hamilton. During his administra-
> tion occurred the war with Tripoli, the Louisiana Purchase, the
> reduction of the national debt, etc. He retired to his seat at
> Monticello in Virginia and died, as did John Adams, on Inde-
> pendence Day, July 4, 1826.

What an historical coincidence, these two friends passing away
on the anniversary of the day they signed the Declaration of Inde-

10

pendence! Wrote John Milton, "Death is the golden key that opens the palace of eternity." The brilliant Goethe's last words, as he passed to his reward in 1832, were, "Give me light." May more of us than now be aware of and blest by the enlightenment that graced these two who shared in the founding of the greatest nation that ever existed!

Speaking of power over others, my long-time associate, Reverend Edmund Opitz, wrote: "Never advocate any more power for your best friends, than you would willingly see wielded by your worst enemies." He would be pleased rather than offended if I rejected his wielding of power over me. The appropriate alternative? We work together by aiding each other.

Jefferson's phrase, "power over others," had to do with organized police force, politicians running the lives of others. In a word, coercion—a form of slavery. The world's largest quotation book—nearly 3,000 pages, everything from "ability" to "zeal," omits this slavish word, "coercion." That English philosopher, Herbert Spencer, (1820–1903) gave the answer: "What is essential to the idea of a slave? We primarily think of him as one who is owned by another. . . . That which fundamentally distinguishes the slave is that he labours under coercion to satisfy another's desires. . . . What . . . leads us to qualify our conception of the slavery as more or less severe? Evidently the greater or smaller extent to which effort is compulsorily expended for the benefit of another instead of self-benefit."

Thomas Jefferson, who wrote into the Declaration of Independence ". . . that all men are *endowed by their Creator* with certain unalienable rights," were he to look down upon our present situation, would be flabbergasted, dismayed, shocked.

The idea of Creator-endowed rights is nonsense to atheists. To them, there is nothing beyond man's earthly sojourn. There is no

Heaven! However, evidence to the contrary has been growing for the past 2,000 years. I know it to be a fact!

What would shock our national hero more than anything else would be the millions of nonrational beings getting enjoyment from *the exercise of power over others.*

Edmund Burke had some thoughts on power:

Power gradually extirpates from the mind every humane and gentle virtue.

The greater the power, the more dangerous the abuse.

A few others:

Power tends to corrupt, and absolute power corrupts absolutely.
                                                —*Lord Acton*

Power will intoxicate the best hearts, as wines the strongest heads. No man is wise enough, nor good enough, to be trusted with unlimited power.           —*Caleb C. Colton*

The basis of international anarchy is men's proneness to fear and hatred. This is also the basis of economic disputes, for the love of power, which is at their root, is generally an embodiment of fear. Men desire to be in control because they are afraid that the control of others will be used unjustly to their detriment.
                                                —*Bertrand Russell*

Finally, how does a rational being achieve happiness? Happiness is neither within us only, nor without us; it is the union of ourselves with *Creation:* Infinite Consciousness. While we finite beings can never approximate a union with the *Infinite,* we can continuously strive toward that goal. There is no greater source of joyousness!

The happiest life is that which constantly exercises and educates what is constructively unique in each of us. No two of us have an identical competence; indeed, each changes from day to day. It is this millions time millions of varying abilities which make the free and unfettered market a requirement for successful lives.

Is it by riches, or by virtues, that we are made happy? Wealth's real role is to relegate mundane affairs into the past tense, that we may concentrate on living virtuous lives!

Happiness can be built *only on virtue,* not on power over others. The joyful life must, of necessity have for its foundation *the seeking of truth!*

# 4

# RIGHTEOUSNESS LEADS TO HAPPINESS

*Happiness consists in the attainment
of our desires, and in having only
right desires.* —**SAINT AUGUSTINE**

Saint Augustine, Bishop of Hippo, wrote his autobiography entitled *Confessions* about 16 centuries ago. I am reliably informed that this gem has been and still is the most widely read autobiography ever written. People respond to excellence in another.

Here, in this exemplary man's story, we see how the law of attraction works its wonders. The lesson for those of us who work for liberty? Get so excellent in understanding and explaining the freedom philosophy that others will seek one's tutorship. Anyone out front in any field, be it golf, astronomy or whatever, exerts an attractive force. A noted astronomer, Anthony Standen, wrote this enlightening statement:

> All the phenomena of astronomy, which had baffled the acutest minds since the dawn of history, the movement of the heavens,

of the sun and the moon, the very complex movement of the planets, suddenly tumble together and become intelligible in terms of the one staggering assumption, this mysterious "*attractive force.*" And not only the movements of heavenly bodies, far more than that, the movement of earthly bodies, too, are seen to be subject to the same mathematically definable law, instead of being, as they were for all previous philosophers, mere unpredictable happen-so's.[1]

It is my contention that the same law applies to human bodies as to the astronomical "earthly bodies," the law of gravitation being one of many examples. Standen may have meant this; in any event, I believe he would agree.

True, happiness comes from having only *right* desires. But first, it is important to reflect on the despondency that results from *wrong* desires: indifference, covetousness, lust, fame.

Indifference never wrote great works, nor thought out striking inventions, nor reared the solemn architecture that awes the soul, nor breathed sublime music, nor painted glorious pictures, nor undertook heroic philanthropies. All of these and other grandeurs are never born of indifference.

The English divine, Robert South, wrote this on covetousness: "The covetous person lives as if the world were made altogether for him, and not he for the world; to take in everything and part with nothing."

While many people deplore covetousness, few will compare it to murder, theft, adultery as an evil. Nor will they think of it as having any bearing on our current politico-economic problem. This wrong assessment may be due to the fact that "Thou shalt not covet" brings up the rear of the Mosaic thou-shalt-nots.

---

[1]See *Science Is a Sacred Cow* by Anthony Standen (New York: E. P. Dutton & Co., Inc., 1950), pp. 63–64.

I suspect that the ordering of the Commandments had nothing to do with a sin-grading plan. Only one of the ten has obvious priority and it became the First Commandment. The next eight Commandments deal with conduct; they enjoin certain overt actions and forbid others. The Tenth Commandment deals with an inner attitude, a state of mind; it is more subtle than the other nine. But if we reflect on the matter, we realize that covetousness is just as deadly as the other sins—indeed, it is a spiritual defect that tends to induce the others.

Covetousness or envy generates a destructive radiation with ill effect on all it touches; it is a canker of the soul. Psychosomatic illness can be traced as much to envy as to hate, anger, worry, despondency.

But consider the social implications, the effects of envy on others. At first blush, the rich man appears not to be harmed because another covets his wealth. Envy, however, is not a benign, dormant element of the psyche; it has the same intensive force as rage, and a great deal of wisdom is required to put it down. Where understanding and self-control are lacking, the weakling will resort to thievery, embezzlement, piracy, even murder, to gratify his envy and "get his share."

The English Quaker and American Colonist and founder of Pennsylvania, William Penn (1644–1718) grasped the point: "Covetousness is the greatest of Monsters, as well as the root of all Evil."

When it is clear that covetousness thwarts Creation's purpose and, thus, man's destiny—that among the cardinal sins none is more dangerous—it surely behooves each of us to find a way to rid his or her self of this evil. I believe the way is simple to proclaim: *Count your blessings!* There is no room for covetousness in the heart filled with gratitude.

Now to *lust,* a vice akin to covetousness—"greed . . . piggishness." Wrote the Roman naturalist, Pliny The Elder (23–79): "Lust is an enemy of the purse, a canker to the mind, a corrosive to the conscience, a weakness of the wit, a besotter [a stupefier] of the senses and, finally, a mortal bane of all the body."

Lust stifles reason and puts passions on the rampage; the irrationality it begets is an enemy of the free and unfettered market. The victims seldom seek counsel from those who have some truth to share. Lust is, indeed, a hellish malady of the mind.

While there are ever so many derogatory habits, I shall conclude the negative phase of this commentary with *fame*—a passion for notoriety at the expense of righteousness. Wrote the Scottish author, Robert Louis Stevenson (1850–94): "It is for fame that men do brave actions; They are only silly fellows after all."

Anyone who seeks fame by doing harm to his fellow men, by robbing Peter to pay Paul, or by countless other infractions of righteousness, is ignoble. Such actors fall into the "silly fellows" category. The antonym for bravery is "craven or cowardly;" traits which are infamous.

Finally, to "Happiness consists of having *only right desires.*" Wrote the English philosopher, Thomas Hobbes (1588–1679): "Our nature is inseparable from desires, and the mere word desire—the *craving* for something not possessed—implies that our present felicity is not complete."

What are the right desires? There are many answers to this question, and each person must draw up his own list. Here is part of mine:

- A desire to grow, day-in-and-day-out, in consciousness, that is, in the perfection of self.
- A desire to know our countless blessings.

- A desire to recognize the mystery of Creation at the Heavenly and earthly levels.
- A desire to better understand and explain the freedom way of life.
- A desire to share one's ideas with all who care to listen.
- A desire to recognize that no matter how far we advance, our felicity is never complete.

Happiness can be built only on virtue, and must of necessity *have truth for its foundation.*

# 5

# AFLAME WITH RIGHTEOUSNESS

*Some nations ... once they have
grown prosperous lose interest in
freedom and let it be snatched from
them without lifting a hand to defend it, lest they should endanger
thus the comforts that, in fact, they
owe to it alone. It is easy to see that
what is lacking in such nations is a
genuine love of freedom, that lofty
aspiration which (I confess) defies
analysis. For it is something one must
feel and logic has no part in it.*
        **—ALEXIS DE TOCQUEVILLE**


From the earliest years of our history America prospered. Other
nations of the world whose soils were as fertile and climates as
friendly as the U.S.A. were poverty-stricken and they wondered
why America flourished. Many governments sent commissions
here to find the answer. All returned to their homelands with the
wrong answers. It was only that French statesman, Tocqueville
(1805–59) who, when visiting here, found the right answer:

> I sought for the greatness and genius of America in fertile fields
> and boundless forests; it was not there. I sought for it in her free

schools and her institutions of learning; it was not there. I
sought for it in her matchless constitution and democratic congress; it was not there. Not until I went to the churches of
America and found them aflame with righteousness did I understand the greatness and genius of America. America is great
because America is good. When America ceases to be good,
America will cease to be great.[1]

*And logic has no part in it.* I am reminded of Charles F. Kettering's remark: "Logic is an organized way of going wrong with
confidence."

No question about it, our Constitution was excellent as was the
Bill of Rights. These documents limited government more than
governments had ever been limited in any nation.[2] Result? No
citizen turned to government for help and for two reasons: (1) it
had nothing on hand to give, and (2) it had not the power to take
from some and give to others. For more than ten decades a self-
responsible, self-reliant citizenry!

Constitutions, however, short of a perpetual righteousness, lose
their discipline and fade away as has ours. A good example is
Argentina. A commission from that nation came here along with
other commissions from other countries. On returning, they wrote
a Constitution even better than ours. Have a look at Argentina
today. In a deplorable politico-economic mess!

---

[1]This quotation is found on pages 12–13 of the popular school text by F. A.
Magruder, *American Government: A Textbook on the Problems of Democracy.*
Except for the last two sentences, this is Magruder's paraphrase of Tocqueville's
words.

[2]"No one can read our Constitution without concluding that the people who
wrote it wanted their government severely limited; the words 'no' and 'not' employed in restraint of governmental power occur 24 times in the first seven articles
of the Constitution and 22 more times in the Bill of Rights." ("Liberty and Ethical
Values," Edmund A. Opitz)

In the spring of 1940 I paid my first visit to Argentina. It was then one of the world's most prosperous nations. Why? They were adhering more or less to free market principles. Three pesos was equivalent to a 1940 dollar. In any event, free-market thinking lapsed. Result? A Command Society! What has happened to the peso's value? A brilliant Argentinean—a freedom devotee—recently bought four cups of coffee in Buenos Aires and remarked to his friends, "I am paying more pesos for the coffee today than I paid for a new automobile in 1936." The lesson? It is only doing what's right—freedom—that matters!

*Some nations . . . once they have grown prosperous lose interest in freedom.* Other wise men agree:

Everything in the world may be endured except continued prosperity.                                               —*Goethe*

"Everything" is too strong a term, for there are other things than prosperity that some people cannot endure. For instance, how hard it is for a politician—as distinguished from a statesman—to endure the thought of citizens acting freely and creatively as they please? Why? Fat-headedness—be-like-me-ness—rules their despicable conduct!

Prosperity has this property, it puffs up *narrow* souls, makes them imagine themselves high and mighty, and they look down upon the world with contempt.                    —*Sophocles*

He that swells in prosperity will be sure to shrink in adversity.
                                                        —*Caleb Colton*

A swelled head is incapable of coping with adversity. Those who have not known ill fortune are lacking in knowledge of themselves, and they are ignorant of their potential virtues as well. As to such citizens, Tocqueville wrote, ". . . they lose interest in freedom and let it be snatched from them without lifting a hand to defend it." They cannot defend freedom, and for a simple reason: they are too low on the politico-economic ladder. Most of them, resorting to legal plunder, are in a know-nothing category.

*. . . lest they should endanger thus the comforts that, in fact, they owe to it alone.* Wrote the Scottish clergyman, Samuel Rutherford: "Of all created comforts, God is the leader, you are the borrower, not the owner."

One of my prayers is: "Blessings upon our associates, near and far, past and present; the perfection of our ideas and ideals; our adherence to them; and our faith in Thee." Admittedly, I am a borrower, not the owner!

Descend to my level. We mortals, at best, possess no more than finite consciousness. Is creativity within our range? Yes, indeed! It comes by way of a strict adherence to private ownership, the free market, and government limited to keeping the peace and invoking a common justice; briefly, everyone free to act creatively as he or she pleases. We owe all laudable comforts to freedom!

Finally, does freedom defy analysis? Yes, we only know that it works, not how the trillions of miracles configurate and confer their countless blessings. However, we can *feel* this phenomenon. Thanks, Alexis de Tocqueville, for grasping *the wonders of early America!*

# 6

# FAITH GONE TO WORK

*Holiness is religious principle put into action. It is faith gone to work. It is love coined into conduct; devotion helping human suffering, and going up in intercession to the great source of all good.*
**—FREDERICK D. HUNTINGTON**

The above thoughts by an American clergyman (1819–1904) deserve some serious reflection. Here are a few of mine which I take pleasure in sharing.

*Faith gone to work.* For our work toward the restoration of freedom to be effective we must believe in our cause. As Goethe wrote, "Miracle is the darling child of faith."

The turnabout from our growing socialism to the freedom way of life appears to fall in the miracle category. But we must believe it will happen or our doubts will postpone it to a far distant future.

As the flower is before the fruit, so is faith before good works.
*—Richard Whately*

In actual life every great enterprise begins with and takes its first step in faith.                    —*August Schlegel*

Faith makes the discords of the present the harmonies of the future.                              —*Robert Collyer*

All I have seen teaches me to trust the Creator for all I have not seen.                                   —*Emerson*

*It is love coined into conduct.* Wrote Shakespeare: "Love works not with the eyes but with the mind." Our finite minds cannot grasp Infinite Truth. Our role? Go forward step by step—from light to light. If our conduct be right, then the paralyzing fear of socialistic disaster will not plague us. We find in John IV:18 the formula: *Perfect love casteth out fear.*

. . . *devotion helping human suffering.* There are two ways to aid those who are in distress, suffering from the lack of food and clothing and other life-sustaining items. The first is the practice of Judeo-Christian charity—voluntary assistance. When governments pre-empt the practice of philanthropy—food stamps, social security and other "welfare" measures—the practice of private charity is dramatically abandoned. If a neighbor is starving, most citizens say, "That's the government's job." Rid ourselves of this political nonsense and nearly everyone would share his or her last loaf of bread.

Charity, when properly practiced, has two disciplines: (1) never let the recipient be aware of the source and (2) let the giver take no personal credit for the gift—that is, avoid self-conceit. It works wonders![1]

The second way to alleviate distress is as much a mystery to most citizens as the appropriate practice of charity. What is the

---

[1] I am unaware of any explanation on this point so enlightening as in *Magnificent Obsession,* a book by Lloyd Douglas (Boston: Houghton Mifflin, 1938).

real road to success so rarely believed? It is the free and unfettered market with government limited *strictly* to keeping the peace and invoking a common justice—no exception, none whatsoever, dictocrats in the past tense!

Why this blindness to freedom? 'Tis a megalomania: "a mental disorder characterized by delusions." What is this popular delusion? The populace listens to the countless politicians rather than to the few statesmen. These know-it-alls, utterly unaware of how little they know, promise a heaven on earth and the millions are thus deluded.

There is a remedy for this delusion-egomania syndrome but it is no less difficult to grasp than appropriate charity or how freedom works its wonders. Freedom cannot be sold but only understood by an individual who really wishes to know. Here is my answer: *The more one understands the more his awareness grows of how much there is to understand.* There are others who share this view—three samples:

The first step to knowledge is to know we are ignorant.
                                                        —*Richard Cecil*

He fancies himself enlightened, because he sees the deficiencies of others; he is ignorant, because he has not reflected on his own.                                                —*Bulwer*

Fullness of knowledge always and necessarily means some understanding of the depths of our ignorance, and that is always conducive to both humility and reverence.   —*Robert Millikan*

When and if enough citizens become aware of their finite nature—how very limited their understanding of themselves, and thus of every other human being, past and present, our millions of dictocrats—know-it-alls—will become "dead-give-away-ers," an appropriate slang expression. And then? The enlightenment: freedom, tiny bits of creative expertise freely flowing to the benefit of one and all!

. . . *and going up in intercession* [*mediation*] *to the great source of all good.* What this means is improving as a go-between—advancing in an understanding of The Divine Source and sharing with those who care to listen. God is one of the names which we give to that eternal, infinite and incomprehensible Source. My reference is always to Infinite Consciousness for it is a reality now and forever.

George Washington saw the light: *"Labor to keep alive in your heart that little spark of celestial fire called conscience."*

# 7

# OUR HOPED-FOR AMERICA

> *We want the spirit of America to be efficient; we want American character to be efficient; we want American character to display itself in what I may, perhaps, be allowed to call spiritual efficiency—that clear, disinterested thinking and fearless action along the right lines of thought.*
> **—WOODROW WILSON**

Recently, I read a book published in 1900 entitled *The State*. On page 572 is a statement by *Professor* Woodrow Wilson: "Government, in its last analysis, is organized force," a truism I have been repeating for years.

Governmental power over citizens is a physical force, as is a clenched fist. Find out what the fist can and cannot do and we will know what political force should and should not do.

What can this force do? It can inhibit, restrain, prohibit. What, in all good conscience, should be inhibited, restrained, prohibited?

The answer is so obvious that it has been known for well over 2,000 years: The Commandments forbid us to kill, steal, lie, covet, commit adultery, bear false witness. Briefly, do no evil!

What can the fist, this physical force, not do? It cannot create. The creative force, in all instances, is a spiritual rather than a physical force, in the sense that discoveries, inventions, insights, intuitive flashes are spiritual. Everything by which we live has its origin in the spiritual before it shows forth in the material. A glass, for instance, is inconceivable had not some cave dweller eons ago discovered how to harness fire. There would be no autos or planes, or any of the countless other material things that grace our lives, had not some Hindu a thousand years ago invented the concept of zero. All modern chemistry, physics, astronomy would be out of the question with only Roman numerals at our disposal. These spiritual forces, since the dawn of consciousness, number in the trillions.

So, how do I draw the line between what government should and should not do? I would have government *limited* to inhibiting and penalizing the destructive actions; leave all creative activities— without exception, education or whatever—to citizens acting freely, cooperatively, competitively, voluntarily, privately.

Professor Wilson wrote; "We want the spirit of America to be efficient; we want American character to be efficient." The spirited person is alert, animated, bright, keen, vivacious. To be efficient means the capacity to achieve desired results with minimum expenditure of energy, time and resources; briefly, competence, expertise, know-how.

The Professor's aspiration? In the year 1900 when he wrote these thoughts, the decline from the American dream had begun: men are endowed to life and liberty by their Creator, not by government. Freedom fading, socialism growing! Woodrow Wilson was praying that more and more Americans would respect and believe in freedom as easily and naturally as our Founding Fathers. We at FEE share these excellent thoughts!

*We want American character to be efficient.* My dictionary defines character as "a distinctive trait, quality or attribute . . . an individual's pattern of behavior or personality; *moral character.*" The American educator, Thomas Dwight Woolsey (1801–89), gave this definition intellectual support. "It is not money, nor is it mere intellect, that governs the world; it is moral character *and* intellect associated with moral excellence." It was the high moral quality of our Founding Fathers that, in large part, accounted for "the land of the free and the home of the brave." A good society without high moral attainments among many of its citizens is unthinkable!

Wrote Goethe: "Talents are best nurtured in solitude; character is best formed in the stormy billows of the world."

The stormy billows of our world—U.S.A. and everywhere—are eliciting a growing comprehension and a better understanding of freedom—priceless talents!

Wrote Elbert Hubbard: "What others say of me matters little, what I myself say and do matters much."

Here is a lesson for those of us who fervently believe in private ownership, the free market and limited government. Suppose we were to be swayed by what the millions think of us: those who endorse social security, tariffs, embargoes, minimum wages, child labor laws, coercive labor union practices—and those who endorse countless economic monstrosities such as the Gateway Arch, built with the earnings of taxpayers! Were we to be guided by what these others think of us, we at FEE would fall in the category of our philosophical adversaries. Cowardly nonsense!

What we say and do matters ever so much. No two individuals

have an identical definition of Truth. Indeed, if one is learning, his or her views are always upgrading. Were no one to agree with Truth as I interpret it, I wouldn't budge an iota. We at FEE believe that everyone—no exception whatsoever—should be free to act creatively as he or she pleases. This is the very essence of freedom!

Goethe used the terms, Nature and God, interchangeably. He had this to say about nonsense and Truth: "Nature understands no jesting; she is always true, always serious, always severe; she is always right, and the errors and faults are always those of man. The man incapable of appreciating her she despises and only to the apt, the pure, and the true, does she resign herself and reveal her secrets." Goethe was a freedom devotee!

Were enough of us to follow Goethe's wisdom we would, as a nation, be blest with what Professor Wilson referred to as "spiritual efficiency." There would, indeed, be a glorious realization of *our hoped-for America!*

# 8

# SPARKED WITH PERSONAL LIBERTY

*Without the wide diversification of talents, taste, abilities and ambitions that now and always exist among men, Society could neither feed nor clothe itself. It is consequently a wise provision of Providence that causes the perpetuation of endless variety in the desire and capabilities of human beings.* Sparked with personal liberty *and the natural personal incentive to own property and to advance economically, this conglomeration of inequality synchronizes into a great engine for the sustenance and progress of mankind.*

**—CLARENCE MANION**

The late Clarence Manion was Dean, School of Law, University of Notre Dame. He retired from that position and began The Manion Forum. By reason of excellent thinking and speaking, he gained the friendship of countless freedom devotees. A much published author, his 1951 book, *The Key to Peace,* is still available.[1] This is a brilliant study of the religious foundation of our free institutions.

---

[1]Available from FEE (107 pages, $2.00).

Suppose that you and I and our neighbors displayed no diversification, no dissimilarity of talents, tastes, abilities and ambitions—each of us a clone cooped up in his shell. Human oysters might be an apt term for such creatures.

As a matter of fact, it is impossible to conjure up such a picture—of human beings without a wide diversification of talents. Such creatures could not survive; apart from human differences "Society could neither feed nor clothe itself," as Manion points out. All—no exception—would perish.

Wrote Herbert Hoover: "*The spark of liberty* in the mind and spirit of man cannot be long extinguished; it will break into flames that will destroy every coercion which seems to limit it."

In 1928 I lived in Palo Alto and was Manager of its Chamber of Commerce. Across the road, bordering on Stanford University, was Mr. Hoover's lovely home. He had been elected President; the Inauguration was to be on March 4, 1929. I organized a 16-car train of Californians to travel to the nation's capital to honor our hometown friend. We were the first to shake his hand as he entered his office in the White House. From 1940 to the time of his demise in 1964, I called on him ever so many times at his apartment— Waldorf Towers, New York City.

I know not when he wrote the above bit of wisdom but I suspect that it was as a private citizen—before or after he was President— times he devoted to creative thinking, not being immersed in political action!

As explained in another chapter, "The Touchstone of Progress," liberty has been sparked in the minds and hearts of men on numerous occasions during the past five centuries. When it broke into flames—to use Hoover's aphorism—it consumed nearly all coercive, know-it-all idiocies.

However, when this laudable spark dies to the point of impotency, an outside force is needed to bring the latent virtue to a new birth. On what does a new birth depend? Horace, that Roman poet of 2,000 years ago, gave the answer: "Adversity has the effect of eliciting talents which in times of prosperity would have lain dormant."

Challenge and response is in accord with the Cosmic Design: evolution/devolution, now and forever, evolution inching ahead over the millennia. All nations—no exception—have experienced the devolutionary trend, but I am confident that the turnabout is certain. To illustrate: Thirty years ago, in a discussion period following my lecture, one of the participants asked, "Just what socialistic interventions would you remove?" My reply, "I cannot answer that question, but if you were to ask me which I would retain, the answer would be *none*!"

Imagine trying to name all the fallacious practices of our 78,000 governments! No person in a lifetime could discover, let alone name them! This is an indication of how despotic our situation has been.

Return to Manion that we may share his wisdom: "This conglomeration of *inequality* synchronizes into *a great engine* for the sustenance and progress of mankind."

Inequality—each individual different from all others and self-different from moment to moment—is variation. Thank Heaven for this blessing!

Wrote Tryon Edwards: "The highest obedience in the spiritual life is to be able always, and in all things, to say, 'Not my will but thine [Righteousness] be done'." The righteous will leads a person to act in harmony with principles or ends. If one has the proper end in view—Freedom—then his principles are right.

Without change there is no progress; but every change upsets accustomed ways of doing things, so we resist. We are creatures of habit, which is why things get stuck on dead center. Over the past half century, for example, we have become so accustomed to the New Deal style of life that governmental regulation of the economy feels like the American Way.

But there are those who refuse to go along with things as they are, nonconformists out of step with the prevailing consensus, people who strive for better ways of doing things. Without such people the world would show little progress, and freedom would wither.

As Kettering wrote, "The world hates change, yet it is the only thing that has brought progress." I would add, it is the only thing that ever will. And if we are open to life the change may occur unexpectedly. Paul's letter to the Corinthians describes the process: *we shall all be changed, in a moment, in the twinkling of an eye*.

# 9

# EXERTING A USEFUL INFLUENCE

*He who wishes to exert a useful influence must be careful to insult nothing. Let him not be troubled by what seems absurd, but concentrate his energies to the creation of what is good. He must not demolish but build. He must raise temples where mankind may come and partake of the purest pleasures.* **—GOETHE**

What did the great Goethe mean by the admonition that you, I or anyone, wishing to exert a *useful* influence, "must be careful to insult nothing"? The meaning of insult is to "affront, outrage, degrade, debase." His reference was not to disagreement but to verbal slaughter. We of the freedom faith—Goethe being outstanding—do not agree with communists but we only damage our way of life and thus ourselves by filthy name-calling. Away with this derogatory tactic!

*Let him not be troubled by what seems absurd.* The English poet, Alexander Pope (1688–1744) gave a good reason for not being troubled: "To pardon those absurdities in ourselves which we condemn in others, is neither better nor worse than to be more willing to be fools ourselves than to have others so."

Reflect on the numerous politicians, and those not in office, who condemn the freedom philosophy and at the same time never give a thought to the absurdities of socialism which they so heartily sponsor. We would, indeed, be fools were we to pardon defects in ourselves or others which we believe to be contrary to liberty for one and all! Socialism is foolishness; freedom is wisdom. Stand for a righteous freedom regardless of the opposition. Let the others be foolish but not those of us who are freedom devotees!

*. . . but concentrate his energies to the creation of what is good.* Wrote the English philosopher, A. A. C. Shaftsbury (1671–1713): "To love the public, to study universal good and to promote the interest of the whole world, as far as it lies within our power, is the height of goodness and makes the temper which we call divine."

To do good is man's most glorious undertaking but, as Thoreau wrote, "Be not merely good but be good for something." There is indeed a distinction between ambition and accomplishment.

We who really love the public—the welfare of everyone in the U.S.A.—will strive to understand and to explain *all* inhibitions to their creative actions that such monstrosities may be removed. Our goal? Let all people be free to achieve their unique potentialities, that is, free to produce what they please and to exchange thoughts or products. Briefly, a grand togetherness—ideological and economic!

Why is it so important to strive for creativity at home? Such an endeavor teaches us how we should deal with the whole world.

Production and exchange should be just as free between nations as it ought to be among Americans.

Today, such international freedom is no more than a dream of a very few. Today our ambassadors are *only* from the political realm. Why should representation be so limited? Free traders work for peace among nations, based on voluntary exchanges within nations. Wrote the English novelist, Henry Fielding (1701–84): "There is nothing so useful to man in general, nor so beneficial to particular societies and individuals, as trade. This is that alma mater, at whose plentiful breast, all mankind are nourished."

How make our dreams come true? Emulate that wise observation by the English poet, John Milton (1608–74): "Give me the liberty to know, to think, to believe, and to utter freely, according to conscience, above all other liberties."

*We must not demolish but build.* Wrote Emerson, "Every violation of truth is a stab [injury] at the health of human society." Man is at once an individual and a social being, therefore, each of us should scrupulously avoid declining in either respect. Mind intelligently employed is mind and life enjoyed. A highly developed consciousness is the source of joy!

"To build," as Goethe urged, one must begin building "castles in the air," as the saying goes. Thoreau wrote: "If you have built castles in the air, your work need not be lost; there is where they should be. Now put foundations under them."

To what should we aspire? A freeing of the human spirit; the millions of American citizens no longer wards of our more or less 78,000 governments. What then? Growing, emerging, self-responsible citizens, each his own man or woman. Castles in the air? Let us build foundations under those worth keeping!

*We must raise temples where mankind may come and partake of the purest pleasures.* The clergyman, William Mountford (1816–

85), wrote: "Often and often to me, and instinctively, has an innocent pleasure felt like a foretaste of infinite delight, an antepast of heaven. Nor can I believe otherwise than that pure happiness is of a purifying effect; like the manna from heaven, no doubt it is meant to invigorate as well as to gratify."

Let us raise temples in which an increasing number of us may *worship the truth of freedom!*

# 10

# OPPORTUNITY: THE GREAT ART OF LIFE?

*To improve the golden moment of opportunity and catch the good that is within our reach, is the great art of life.* —SAMUEL JOHNSON

While I agree with Johnson, there are numerous exceptions which warrant the question mark in my title, an example being furnished by the English divine, Isaac Watts (1674–1748): "Life is a long tragedy, this globe the stage." In view of the fact that the best among us never complain about the lack of opportunities, it seems appropriate to reflect on these countless blessings.

A formula for a successful life is to be ready for any and all opportunities which are in harmony with our capabilities or talents. No two persons, past or present, are identical in this respect. Indeed, each individual, when striving for improvement, changes from day to day. Up to age thirty five, I had more than a dozen occupations, all of which I abandoned—disharmonious! Further, on four occasions I was offered jobs with salaries four to five times what I was receiving. Refused! I finally found my occupational niche: the love of liberty and a craving to better understand and explain this way of life. So far, nearly fifty years of joyous work.

Suppose that everyone else had a goal identical to mine and worked at nothing else. All would perish! There would be no food or housing or countless other necessities of life.

A fact shocking to most individuals: all would perish were there no freedom! Why does this give the appearance of contradicting historical facts? People survived under the reign of Hitler, Stalin, Mussolini and numerous others of this despicable ilk. The explanation: there were at least two reasons, (1) disobedience and (2) goods and services traded with people in productive nations.

To grasp the point, merely imagine that no citizen of these unfortunate nations could produce or exchange anything which their dictocrat did not specify. Such a fathead couldn't even manage the lives of his few neighbors, let alone the millions unknown to him or their talents and opportunities. It is self-evident that all would perish including the know-it-all!

Here is an excellent metaphor—figure of speech—by Shakespeare:

> There is a tide in the affairs of men, which, taken at the flood, leads on to fortune; omitted, all the voyage of their life is bound in shallows and in miseries; and we must take the current when it serves, or lose our ventures.

Meaning? In history's ups and downs, dating back to the Sumerians of about 4,500 years ago, there have been several freedom-oriented civilizations, the greatest of all being the U.S.A., as designed by our Founding Fathers.[1]

---

[1]For details see "Eruptions of Truth," a chapter in my book, *Awake for Freedom's Sake*.

Those familiar with the Bard of Avon's thinking know that he was not referring to pounds or dollars or any other monetary unit by the word "fortune." What then? Truth—Righteousness. For confirmation: ". . . to thine own self be true, And it must follow, as the night the day, Thou canst not then be false to any man."

. . . *omitted, all the voyage of their life is bound in shallows and in miseries; and we must take the current when it serves, or lose our ventures.* Most of our miseries come from a want of courage to speak the truth, as one sees it or, worse yet, to have no inkling of truth, or love of it. Life's worthwhile ventures at a dead end!

Wrote the American author, Bayard Taylor (1825–78): "Opportunity is rare, and a wise man will never let it go by him." As already noted, opportunities are indeed rare in countries where one cannot act creatively as he or she pleases. Rare, too, are opportunities for you or me that are beyond the range of our potentialities or talents. Astronomy is no more within my range than is the making of an ordinary wooden lead pencil.[2] And, all too rare are the astronomers—or those who have a part in pencil-making and countless other specializations—who strive for an understanding of human liberty. The wise individual will never "let it go by him."

Wrote Christina, the Queen of Sweden (1626–89): "It is necessary to try to surpass one's self *always;* this occupation ought to last as long as life." What an insight, a revelation that goes to the very root of human destiny—the wellspring of what man is intended to become! Wrote Tryon Edwards, "Thoughts lead us to purposes; purposes go forth in action; actions form habits; habits form character; and character fixes our destiny." The hope of an

---

[2]See my brevity, "I, Pencil." Copy on request.

improving America rests on improving characters and the road to this exemplarity is to surpass one's self every day of mortal life!

An excellent thought by the American clergyman, William Ellery Channing (1780–1842): "The office of government is not to confer happiness, but to give men *equal opportunity* to work out happiness for themselves." Note the ways that governments—federal, state and local (approximately 78,000 of them)—strive to impose their stupid ideas of happiness on us. There are more than anyone knows. A few samples: social security, food stamps, local swimming pools, government financed "educational institutions," ventures into outer space.

Citizens by the millions are victims of a false happiness when they observe flights into outer space. Why false? No one, in or out of government, knows the cost. A hundred billion dollars is doubtless an underestimation. Now, suppose there could be no such flights into fancy except financing by *voluntary* donations. What would the revenue be? Relatively nothing! I, for one, wouldn't give a dime. I would spend my money for ventures that bring happiness to me. Doubtless, most others would do the same. Equal opportunity for one and all!

Wrote B. C. Forbes: "Opportunity knocks as often as a man has an ear trained to hear her, an eye trained to see her, and a head trained to utilize her."

The great art of life, equal opportunity, is, indeed, within our reach: *freedom for one and all!*

# 11

# THE TRIUMPH OF CIVILIZATION

*It is the triumph of civilization that at last communities have ordained such a mastery over natural laws that they drive and control them. The winds, the water, electricity, all aliens that in their wild form were dangerous, are now controlled by human will, and are made useful servants.*
**—HENRY WARD BEECHER**

This New York clergyman, Henry Ward Beecher, (1813–87) lived during the period when the American dream approached closest to realization. Beecher observed in this nation the greatest triumph of civilization in all history. Natural laws represent the original constitution of things, and are thus properly ascribed to Creation itself.

The English divine, Sydney Smith (1771–1845) gave to posterity this excellent thought: "Whatever you are by nature, keep to it; never desert your own line of talent. Be what nature intended you for, and you will succeed."

To say that nature—Creation at the human level—had a million different kinds of talent at her disposal would be a gross under-statement. Shakespeare grasped the point, "O, the difference of man and man!" Life depends on the diversity of talents displayed by people generally. Were everyone the same as you or me, all would perish. Variety is the very spice of life!

Individual freedom of choice is the necessary counterpart to individual variation if the observed diversity of talents is to enrich life. Reflect on countries where the stifling of talents rules the political way of life and stifles the individual. Except for the communist commissars, and their appointed accomplices, who do as they please, no other Russians have genuine freedom of choice. For example, a potential inventive genius may be coercively assigned to sweeping the streets or digging ditches. With creativity squelched, millions live in abject poverty. To break the dictatorial commands is to incur the death penalty or consignment to Siberia. Woe betide any vocal pro-freedom Russian!

India affords another case in point. On the two occasions when I lectured there I found little understanding of the freedom way of life. A great friend, the late Professor B. R. Shenoy, knew the philosophy well, but he stood almost alone. There was a small pro-freedom organization headquartered in Calcutta. And there was doubtless a remnant here and there unknown to me or even to one another. Otherwise, few listeners or learners—only a fraction of the people aware of the potential of the free way of life. The consequence in India has been and is starvation on a major scale.

Yes, doubtless there was and still is a remnant in India but the number of those who seek them out must be close to zero. Why? A widespread unawareness of how these persons of intellectual attractiveness work their wonders. In the public eye are the do-gooders—those who would reform others—make carbon copies of themselves.

Members of the effective Remnant are few in number, and no others really count. The Remnant are, as Albert Jay Nock observed, an odd lot, quiet, shy of show-offs, indeed, they will have nothing to do with such types. These few—mostly unknowns—*are the ones who tip the scales,* and their search is always for those who, to some extent, make progress against their own bewilderment, who gain in understanding and clarity of expression, who evidence integrity and, above all, who strive to enlighten themselves. Those of The Remnant "run a mile" from reformers, they resent all attempts at "ramming ideas down their necks." This attests to their realism for they know the futility of such an effort. It simply cannot be done.

The Remnant is dramatized in "Isaiah's Job" by Albert Jay Nock. I read this essay 44 years ago. It gave me my first instruction in the methods appropriate to freedom. Like the Bible, from which the story is taken, it merits reading again and again.[1]

True, as Beecher pointed out, there was a time centuries ago when natural forces—the winds, water, electricity—all aliens in their wild form, were dangerous to man. And in Beecher's time, prior to our plague of socialism, the forces were "controlled by human will and are made useful servants." Freedom of choice in the driver's seat!

A commentary on aircraft—natural forces harnessed by the human will—may be helpful to emphasize Beecher's point. This prophecy by Lord Tennyson (1809–1892):

> For I dipt into the future, far
>    as human eye could see,
> Saw the Vision of the world and all
>    the wonders that would be;

---

[1] Copy on request.

> Saw the heavens fill with commerce,
>    argosies of magic sails,
> Pilots of the purple twilight, dropping
>    down with costly bales.

Talk about useful servants! Tennyson's imagination caught a glimpse of our modern aircraft, the magic sails being metal wings. His verse appeared in 1842 when flying machines were but a dream.

Leonardo da Vinci (1452–1519) was another of the rare dreamers. He drew sketches of an airplane four centuries before Tennyson's time—but it wouldn't fly. Had a 747 Jet flown over his home during the night, he would have thought the heavens were falling. And, in a sense, he would have been right. Freedom works its Heavenly Wonders in startling ways!

Wrote the American educator, Alexander Meiklejohn: "Human beings should become civilized, that is, so related to each other that their thinking is a concerted attempt to reach common answers to common problems. They should practice a friendliness of the mind. Violence is savagery. Civilization is reasonableness." Violence—all coercion—governmental or otherwise is, indeed, savagery. However, if enough of us are sound in our reasoning,—thinking—then *civilization—freedom—will triumph!*

# 12

# OUR DUTY AND ITS REWARDS

*Try to put well in practice what you already know; and in so doing, you will in good time discover the hidden things which you now inquire about. Practice what you know and it will help to make clear what now you do not know.* **—REMBRANDT**

This Dutchman (1606–1669), "one of the world's most famous painters," gave the above thoughts to posterity, part of what his outstanding success as a painter had taught him. These enlightenments and admonitions are worthy of our seriously pondering.

Every day of everyone's life—from adulthood to old age—there are one or more duties that challenge the intelligence. Failure to recognize these obligations consigns life to mediocrity. Reflect on the mass of humanity thus afflicted. They die on the vine, as the saying goes. Wrote the French essayist, Montaigne, "It is not death, it is dying that alarms me." The millions thus stalemated are happy in their doldrums, not alarmed. Poor souls!

47

Now, what about the few to whom a recognition and the mastery of duties is a joy? Wrote the English novelist, Henry Fielding (1707–1754): "Great joy, especially after a sudden change of circumstances, is apt to be silent, and dwells rather in the heart, than on the tongue."

Duties, as other circumstances, are forever changing. Why this assertion? One's duties change as new and attractive opportunities present themselves. These new occasions are so numerous that were one not to hold his or her tongue, he or she would sound like a mockingbird. Hold one's tongue! Silence is golden! Let our achievements dwell quietly in the heart.

If one has chosen an understanding and explanation of human liberty as the number one duty, he or she will be blest with insights, intuitive flashes, ideas and thoughts from seers, past and present. To the extent that one succeeds in comprehending liberty, to that extent will new and challenging duties grace ever so many others.

> There is no evil we cannot face or fly from, but the consciousness of duty disregarded.                      *—Daniel Webster*

To be free from evil thoughts is one of Creation's greatest gifts. "When evils have become insufferable, they have touched the point of cure." The evils of runaway government—with inevitable inflationary consequences—now approach the insufferable stage. Three of ever so many examples:

- The Federal government owns roughly 42% of our total geography.
- American business spends 130,000,000 man-hours per year filling out governmental forms and that cost is passed directly on to consumers in the form of increased prices.

- In addition to the devastating effect of taxes, government spending beyond its income has generated monetary inflation of such magnitude that our savings have been devalued by more than 60 per cent in the past ten years.

Can we face or fly from these evils? Hardly! They are, indeed, insufferable and, hopefully, we have reached the point of cure. The remedy for this hoped-for turnabout is our duty and *it must not be disregarded!* It is sink or swim, as the saying goes. Let us swim toward liberty!

> Man is not born to solve the problems of the universe, but to find out what he has to do; and to restrain himself within the limits of his comprehension.     *—Goethe*

The last words of Johann Wolfgang von Goethe, as he passed away in 1832, were, "Give me light." Although one of the wisest—most enlightened—humans, past or present, known to me, he had an awareness, as did Socrates, of how "infinitesimal was his wisdom." To use an old aphorism, he "stuck to his last," that is, to those duties within his comprehension.

Obviously, no individual keenly aware of his limitations tries to solve the problems of the universe. Who does then? The millions of politicians—not statesmen—with not a smidgeon of awareness as to how little they know. They "know" how to run the lives of all persons within their towns, counties, states, nations. The truth? They know not how to run their own lives, let alone yours or mine. "To be ignorant of one's ignorance is the malady of ignorance." Our prayer for each day of mortal life should be, "Give us light." There is not enough darkness in the whole world to put out the light of one wee candle. Nor is there enough ignorance in America to put out the light of liberty.

The consideration that human happiness and moral duty are inseparably connected will always continue to prompt me to promote the former by inculcating the practice of the latter.

—*George Washington*

Wrote the English author, Philip Hamerton: "The happiest life is that which constantly exercises and educates what is best in us." Happiness and moral duty are twin experiences and, if life is lived aright, they are, indeed, inseparable.

What *is* best in us? Reflect on this:

Countless the various species of mankind, countless the shades that separate mind from mind; no *general object of desire is known;* each has his will, and each pursues his own.

—*William Gifford*

Human variation is an endowment of Creation, for the survival of the human species is keyed to individual differences. If by some malign miracle every human being suddenly became a carbon copy of every other, we would all perish. The planet earth would revert back to nature; there would be mountains, oceans, rivers, various living forms, but no people.

No universal object of desire, valid for everyone, is known; never has been or ever will be. People differ and so their goals are not the same. This fact is a Heavenly Blessing that diminishes or increases as an understanding of freedom fades or brightens.

A salute to George Washington for giving us a great truth: the source of happiness is an adherence to moral duty!

Duty performed, gives clearness and firmness to faith, and faith thus strengthened through duty becomes the more assured and satisfying to the soul.          —*Tryon Edwards*

Alexis de Tocqueville: "Despotism may govern without faith

but Liberty cannot.'' The millions of dictocrats in the U.S.A. are without faith in liberty. To the contrary, they are obsessed by the fallacious notion that they are supermen, self-anointed to wield a godlike power over others. This is a messianic delusion.

As Rembrandt, the famous painter, suggested, we should diligently practice what we already know. By so doing, we will, sooner or later, be led to explore the next step in our moral and spiritual upgrading, and the next. This is how we grow, and growth, in turn, will reveal to us how infinitesimal is our wisdom. To acknowledge our finitude is to escape from devastating know-it-all-ness!

To improve the lot of mankind, let each of us do his duty, starting with himself, deepening his understanding of the miracles wrought by freedom. *Have faith in liberty!*

# 13

# THE STEPS TO GREATNESS

*The greatest man is he who chooses
the right with invincible resolution;
who resists the sorest temptations
from within and without; who bears
the heaviest burdens cheerfully; who
is calmest in storms and most fearless under menace and frowns; and
whose reliance on truth, on virtue,
and on God, is most unfaltering.*
**—WILLIAM E. CHANNING**

In the above quotation, this American clergyman (1780–1842),
presents the human being in a rare state of perfection—seldom
attained. I am aware of a few—past and present—possessing these
rare qualities. Exemplars par excellence!

How can this exemplarity grace our lives? It serves as a high
goal toward which we should strive day-in-and-day-out. Each improvement in this intellectual and spiritual direction is a step toward greatness. Such progress relates to those who persistently
seek Truth—enlightenment—and excel their fellowmen in this

quest. Briefly, it depends on the few whose wisdom becomes an attractive force. The Perfect Example? Jesus of Nazareth!

The German statesman, Otto von Bismarck (1815–98), wrote: "A really great man is known by three signs: generosity in the design, humanity in the execution, moderation in success."

Generosity does not impoverish; instead, it enriches the lives of those who practice it, as well as the recipients. "Give and it shall be given unto you." Luke 4:38.

As to the enriching of one's humanity, here is a good aphorism: "A man's nature runs either to herbs or weeds, therefore, let him seasonably water the one and destroy the other." Those whose "nature runs to herbs" are the superior persons who are growing from birth to old age. Watering? Exploring the wisdom of seers, those who possess thoughts superior to one's own.

Weeds? Evils symbolized—stupidities, destructive nonsense, know-it-all-ness, destroyers of all that is good or true. The remedy? An ever-improving self provides deliverance from evil. Errors caught in time can and often do show us the way to understanding and high-grade explanations.

As to "moderation in success"—let getting ahead not go to our heads! "Success at first doth many times *undo* men at last." Think of success as a blessing made possible by the countless achievements of others. No one is or ever was able to go it alone!

*The greatest man is he who chooses the right with invincible resolution.* A determination to succeed is half the battle, as Samuel Smiles tells us: "To think we are able is almost to be so; to determine upon attainment is frequently attainment itself; earnest resolution has often seemed to have about it almost a savor of omnipotence."

These thoughts by Smiles reinforce Channing's wisdom. Elbert Hubbard adds an interesting insight: "There is something that is

much more scarce, something finer far; something rarer than ability. It is the ability to recognize ability."

The ability to recognize the ability of a carpenter, singer, sales-
man, comedian and the like is commonplace. But rare is the ability
to recognize those few throughout history who have excelled others in an understanding and explanation of liberty.

*The . . . man who resists the sorest temptation from within and
without.*

> Temptations *without* imply desires *within*. Men ought not to say,
> "How powerfully the devil tempts," but "How strongly I am
> tempted."                                      —*Henry Ward Beecher*

As to temptations *without,* learn to say "No!" Thirty-six years
ago, when the attractiveness of adhering strictly to conscience was
more of a new idea to me, I was invited to spend an evening with
a dozen of the country's leading businessmen. Our purpose was
to discuss the so-called Full Employment Act, then before the
Congress. Most of the talk favored the tactic of opposing the
measure by subterfuge, dealing under the table, so to speak—
repulsive to me. When they finally asked for my view, I hesitated
a moment. To tell them exactly what I thought would do me in,
damage my career—or so I imagined. But, I told them! Never
have I had a more rewarding experience. From that day forward
those twelve were devoted friends, inviting me to counsel time
after time. Why? Integrity!

As to temptations *within:* while it is not dangerous to be honest,
this does not mean that one must necessarily divulge all of his
innermost thoughts. Many doubtless deserve further incubation.
But once a position is taken and expressed, let there be in it no
deviation from conscience.

Imagine that a fair percentage of citizens of this nation were practicing what their highest conscience dictates as right. No man could ever be elevated to public office except as he exemplified integrity. Think what a change this would make in the national scene. Only statesmen; never a charlatan!

*The . . . man who bears his heaviest burdens cheerfully.* Wrote the Roman poet, Ovid, more than 2,000 years ago: "Burdens become light when cheerfully borne." Could it be that the scholar, Channing, was enlightened by Ovid? Perhaps! As Goethe observed, "All truly wise ideas have been thought already thousands of times." The truly wise individual is usually one who is aware of how little he knows, whereas the individual who thinks himself the wisest falls into the foolish category. "Father, forgive them, for they know not what they do." Luke 23:34.

The best way to cope with our burdens? Have fun as we bear those which are necessary, share those borne by our friends, and overcome the rest. Were more of us to enjoy making ever clearer explanations of the present coercive nonsense by our governments, we would be graced with freedom—and soon!

*The man . . . who is calmest in storms and most fearless under menace and frowns.* "Menace," as here used, means "threats, denunciation, intimidation." Anyone who resorts to these common tactics to get his way is ridiculous. Those who are loudest in their threats get what they deserve: nothing but disdain. We freedom devotees who threaten our opponents only strengthen them in their misdeeds, their societal faults. The tactic we should employ? Calmness! Think exclusively of our own improvement and leave faults to the falsifiers. Errors of opinion may be tolerated where reason is left free. "If we would guide by the light of reason, we must let our minds be bold." Let us be fearless in the face of menace and frowns.

*The . . . man whose reliance is on truth, on virtue, on God, is most unfaltering.* Wrote the clergyman, Stopford A. Brooke (1832–1916): "If a thousand old beliefs were ruined in our march to truth we must still march on."

Reflect on the history of mankind and the thousands of beliefs, once held to be true, that have become "old hat"—the flat earth theory, for example, accepted without question for generations. In spite of all dubious beliefs, we are still marching on to new truths.

As to virtue, a former Stanford University president, David Starr Jordan (1851–1931), gave to posterity this wisdom: "Wisdom is what to do next; Virtue is doing it." May more and more be so graced!

> There is but one pursuit in life which it is in the power of all to follow, and of all to attain. It is subject to no disappointments, since he that perseveres makes every difficulty an advancement, and every conquest a victory; and this is the pursuit of virtue. Sincerely to aspire after virtue is to gain her; and zealously to labor after her ways is to receive them.
>
> —*Caleb C. Colton*

Leading a life of virtue, with a reliance on God, are the *steps to greatness and freedom!*

# 14

# THE PURSUIT OF VIRTUE

*No man can purchase his virtue too dear, for it is the only thing whose value must ever increase with the price it has cost us. Our integrity is never worth so much as when we have parted with all to keep it.*
**—CALEB C. COLTON**

As in the case of Burke and several others, I repeatedly quote this English clergyman. Why? Not only was he a virtuous gentleman but he knew how to counsel his contemporaries and future generations as well on the blessings of living the righteous life. Is not the above a super-excellent guideline, one that inspires reflection and the hope of attainment?

Those who are truly virtuous are few in number. Keep in mind that scarcity raises the price of everything. Thus the ONE in a thousand is more likely to be disdained than esteemed—a high price! Yet, is it too dear? The few devoted to righteousness have no price that is too dear for this Heavenly aspiration. This virtue is integrity and the few so graced will, more or less, contribute to future generations the enlightenment—superior thinking—that Colton has shared with us.

I am obliged to take exception to one of the views of Colton: ". . . there is but one pursuit in life which is in the power *of all* to follow, and of all to attain . . . the pursuit of virtue." My thought? There are numerous simple pursuits such as talking and walking which are pursued and easily attainable.

However, the pursuit of virtue, in my view, is not in the power of all to attain; a few, yes, the many millions, no. Why? Virtue is an intellectual, moral and spiritual aspiration far above lowly, workaday goals. Might as well expect the millions to attain an explanation of why the sun shines. Wrote the English Divine, August W. Hare (1792–1834): "They who disbelieve in virtue because man has never been found perfect, might as reasonably deny the sun because it is not always noon."

*Our integrity is never worth so much as when we have parted with all to keep it.* The value of this virtue? It is "precious, priceless." Wrote Emerson: "I cannot find language of sufficient energy to convey my sense of the sacredness of private integrity."

The Sage of Concord, one of the strongest minds and most energetic phrasers of ideas, acknowledged a weakness: an inability to explain the exalted role of integrity in the life of man. In this respect, I find myself with a conviction identical to his, and a similar inability, no less distressing. At least, I am in good company. One is tempted to side with Bernard Dougall: "Integrity was a word he couldn't spell, let alone define." Such is the unawareness of its meaning and importance!

When it comes to listing the virtues, I know only those that are important to me. Integrity is by all means first and foremost. As to the others—charity, intelligence, justice, love and humility—I have no precise ranking. To me they are tied for second place.

Before going further, let me draw my distinction between integrity and wisdom, for these definitions so closely parallel each other:

> Integrity is an accurate reflection in word and deed of whatever one's highest conscience dictates as right. Wisdom is whatever one's highest conscience perceives as truth.

As to the pursuit of virtue, I concede that one's highest conscience may not in fact be right but is as close to righteousness as one can get. Also, one's highest conscience may not be truth but it as nearly approximates wisdom as is within one's reach. Fallibility applies in either case!

People differ in their evaluation of Emerson's philosophy, but all concede that his proclaimed positions, written and oral, were accurate reflections of whatever his highest conscience dictated as righteous. Never, to my knowledge, did he bend to expediency, that is, resort to deviation from conscience to gain favor or popularity with others. So rigorous were his spiritual convictions that he was at odds with the numerous religious orthodoxies and took no pains to conceal his innermost sentiments. Attuned to his conscience, he stood ramrod straight. As this rare posture is sometimes phrased, he sought approval from God, not men. Integrity!

Yet, Emerson, conscious of the sacredness of integrity, could find no words energetic enough to convey his sense of its importance. In the light of his genius as a thinker and a phraser of ideas, why his confessed inability to handle this concept? Why could he not explain his meaning of integrity to others?

As I see it, the answer lies in one of his own words, the *sacredness* of integrity. This virtue is in a moral and spiritual realm so far above normal experience that we possess no words to portray its meaning. It borders on the Infinite and, thus, is beyond our working vocabulary. This explains why it is so seldom included among the virtues. For these reasons, I am convinced that integrity cannot be taught, at best, it can only be caught. And, then, only by those who devoutly wish to be so graced!

To whom do we look for growth or improvement in the higher realm of thought? Only people of integrity! Those individuals who pay no heed to conscience are forever the victims of expediencies; they are governed by fickle opinions, pressures, mass sentiments, a desire for momentary acclaim. Wisdom—whatever one's highest conscience perceives as truth—is out of range simply because integrity is not observed!

The above should be reason enough to strive for integrity. However, by far the most important reason remains: it is *sacredness*. Though new to me, I now discover that this idea was perceived nearly 2,000 years ago: "The light of the body is the eye: if therefore thine eye be single, thy whole body shall be full of light." (Matthew 6:22) In other words, the light of the body is truth, wisdom, enlightenment. The eye is perception. And what is the meaning of "if thine eye be single"? Refer to Webster for the definition of "single" as here used: "Not deceitful or artful, simple, honest, sincere." Shakespeare used the word in this sense: "I speak with a single heart."

*Single,* in this sense, is directly linked with *integer,* meaning "Whole, entire, not divided." Contrasted to *single* is *double,* which has the same original root as the word, "duplicity." Such phrases as "double-dealing" and "double-talk" convey this connotation. *Integrity* is related to *integer:* and single as here used, refers to integrity.

Phrased in modern idiom, Matthew's insight would read as follows:

Enlightenment of the intellect and spirit of man depends on his powers of perception. If these powers be free from duplicity, that is, if they be grounded in pure integrity, man will be as much graced with enlightenment—wisdom—as is within his capability.

Whatever the mysterious Universal Power—the radiant energy that flows through all life—it is blocked, cut off, stifled by duplicity in any of its forms. Expediency, lying, double talk and the like are ferments of the soul and through which Universal Power does not and cannot flow. "A double-minded man is unstable in all his ways." James I:8.

Only in integrity—when the "eye is single"—do the powers of perception grow, evolve, emerge, hatch. Then the "whole body shall be full of light." Then, and only then, are such virtues as charity, intelligence, justice, love, humility within our reach.

Finally, if we believe that we should not do unto others that which we would not have them do unto us—a concern for others as well as self—we have one more among all the compelling reasons why we should strive first and foremost for integrity.

No one ever gave a better formula for the pursuit of virtue than did the great English economist, John Stuart Mill (1806–73): "It would not be easy, even for an unbeliever, to find a better translation of the rule of virtue from the abstract into the concrete, than to endeavor so to live that Christ would approve our life." Conformity to such high standards of conduct would, when voluntary, do away with wrongdoing and vice. Were enough of us to pursue this high order of virtue, we would assure *the highest order of freedom!*

# 15

# THE UNFOLDING LIFE

*Height is our aim, not because of any man-made doctrine about height and ascension, but because the universal processes everywhere indicate height as the aim of all unfolding life. Yet, in the pursuit of this end, there is no escape from the natural process of growth.*     **—NEWTON DILLAWAY**

Ralph Waldo Emerson (1803–82), known as the Sage of Concord, began school at the age of two and became famous for his independent thinking. In December, 1975, I read Newton Dillaway's book, *The Gospel of Emerson*.

A bit of background may help account for my favorable review of this remarkable book. Sometime earlier, an English friend, one of the most scholarly and brilliant men of my acquaintance, startled me with, "Leonard, you are the most religious person I have ever known." Nonplused, indeed, for I had always thought of myself as rather far down the line in this phase of life. I did not know what he was driving at. Later my friend asked who were my favorite philosophers. I gave him several names beginning with Emerson. His response, "I now know why I think of you as so religious."

No subject has had more reflection than religion and none has produced a greater diversity of conclusions. They range all the way from the findings of Himalayan yogis to Augustine's *Confessions*. And the employers have ranged from the lowly fisherman of Galilee to the greatest minds of all time, from small fry to big shots, from so-called commoners to the acclaimed elite, from the likes of me to popes. And among them all I have never come upon one more spiritual and religious than the notable and quotable Ralph Waldo Emerson. In my 27 books I have quoted him far more than any other. I quote Emerson and others the better to express myself.

Now to my point. The thoughts of this earthly hero of mine did not fit into any of our numerous orthodoxies. Religion to him was a growing, evolutionary, evolving phase of the individual human spirit. He rejected any and all "this-is-it" propositions. Here is an abbreviation of this phase of his gospel:

Thou shalt not profess that which thou dost not believe.

Thou shalt not heed the voice of men when it agrees not with the voice of God in thine own soul.

Thou shalt study and obey the laws of the Universe, and they will be thy fellow servants.

Nature shall be to thee as a symbol. The life of the soul in constant union with the Infinite shall be for thee the only real existence.

Teach men that each generation begins the world afresh, *in perfect freedom;* that the present is not the prisoner of the past, but that today holds captive all the yesterdays, to judge, accept, to reject their teachings, as they are shown by its own morning sun.

Emerson kept a Journal during his adult life—recording all of his ideas and ideals. Having kept my own Journal for more than 29 years, never missing a day—now nearing 2,500,000 words—I know the value of such a discipline, namely, the capture of ideas as they flash into mind. Ideas are like dreams—evanescent, vanishing, ephemeral, gone with the wind, as the saying goes.

Now to the late Newton Dillaway, an intimate corresponding friend for some years. I hardly know how to describe his fabulous—"hard to believe, astounding"—insights. Perhaps "esoteric" will suffice: "intended or understood by only a chosen few." Although we had never met face to face, he would write about unbelievable acquaintances with me, a togetherness the likes of which I have never known or suspected. He was on the same intellectual and spiritual ascendancy as Emerson.

Emerson's recordings in his Journal and lectures would doubtless have been lost to posterity had it not been for Dillaway's genius. Let's examine the meaning of "The Unfolding Life." As he writes, "it is height." And height? Heavenward or another term with a comparable meaning: *Excelsior.* Wrote Longfellow:

> The shades of night were falling fast
> As through an Alpine village past
> A youth who bore 'mid snow and ice
> A banner with the strange device,
>   Excelsior!

And speaking of youth and gaining height, the Sage of Concord wrote: "When we converse with what is above us, we do not grow old, but grow young." To be young in spirit is the opportunity to do something and to become somebody.

The following are excerpts from Dillaway's book, *Consent,* with which I wholeheartedly agree.

In the experience of the soul, as in the development of a plant, every "level" must be filled out to achieve health in *all* parts. The attainment of any plane as a natural base involves a slow, steady climb on what Smuts calls "the rugged, upward path of the universe," a release from one state of consciousness to another, one field of magnetic action to another field. The law is that there is no release save in performance.

Epictetus was not teaching "naturalism" in speaking of harmonizing his will with nature. He permitted his will to be used by the universal power, which has its own will, one no man or group of men can reduce to a formula. All we know is that the cosmic will is to be followed, and in health any man will follow it.

But let no one lose sight of the fact that the way of divine acceptance is not the way of formalism, not the way of imposing man-made creeds and doctrines on the universe. That is folly. The universe has its own eternal way and there is no other way in reality.

If you impose limitations on human experience, you block the channels that permit life to flow. The urge to arbitrariness in human nature has been the curse of history, for it is this, more than anything else, that has blocked the flowing and ascension. It has stunted, warped and destroyed the finer elements of human experience.

When a way of life springs from the urge to preserve and promote freedom, it is good. When it springs from the urge to arbitrariness, it is a blockade. It springs also from the urge in man to feel important. If man can "settle things," his vanity is appeased.

Let us learn to lead the unfolding life which is to *grow, aspire, evolve toward freedom!*

# 16

# YIELD NOT TO TEMPTATION

*No one can ask honestly or hope*
*fully to be delivered from temptation*
*unless he has himself honestly and*
*firmly determined to do the best he*
*can to keep out of it.*

—JOHN RUSKIN

The English critic and essayist, John Ruskin (1819–1900), was also known to the public as a social reformer. Doubtless that's what most people would label those few Americans who are presenting the case for freedom as an alternative to the communistic mess into which our country is sinking.[1] But our "reforms" would not be Ruskin's.

For years I have begun one of my lectures with a Ruskin suggestion: "A speaker should always tell his audience where he

---

[1]For the startling extent to which the U.S.A. has adopted the ten points of the *Communist Manifesto,* see the chapter, "Ignorance: Agent of Destruction" in my book, *Vision* (Irvington, N.Y.: The Foundation for Economic Education, 1978), pp. 82–88.

stands at the very outset." So let me tell you where I stand as related to his interventionist philosophy. Wise in ever so many ways, Ruskin believed in mercantilism, no different from our own planned economy and welfare state. I am opposed to every variety of a politically planned economy.

England's Industrial Revolution resulted in an unprecedented prosperity for the English masses. Our own private ownership, free market, limited government way of life resulted in even greater prosperity diffused much more widely. But prosperity breeds a peculiar temptation—the temptation to solicit economic privileges from government. I am acquainted with many Americans, outstanding in their specializations, who seek special privileges—living off others by coercive governmental interventions. They yield to temptation, in some cases unwittingly!

Ruskin's interventionist position has a nonderogatory explanation. To write the above statement and then yield to temptation would make a liar of him. This Englishman was an honest man.

Aware of the enormous bounties that flowed from the Industrial Revolution, Ruskin failed to identify the cause as freedom of choice to act creatively as everyone pleases. To him the event was an historical accident. Millions of honest Americans, unable to see how creation at the human level works its wonders, are also victims of such lack of vision. 'Tis a partial blindness, not temptation, that accounts for this malady.

Creation—Divine Omnipotence—works Its Wonders regardless of human ignorance. As Thomas Alva Edison wrote, "No one knows more than one-millionth of one per cent of anything," and in this lack of understanding we find an explanation for the growing governmental interventions. Politicians—not statesmen—take credit for the bounties Creation has wrought throughout history, and will continue to confer upon humanity.

Wrote the German scholar and ecclesiastic, Thomas à Kempis (1380–1471): "Occasions of adversity best discover how great virtue or strength each one hath. For occasions do not make a man frail, but show what he is."

The present politico-economic adversity is a great teacher for those who seek virtue and truth. Privation strengthens their minds and does, indeed, show what they really are. Why this stimulation? It is an observed fact that acts of overcoming pave the road to becoming—the tremendous power of creative human energy when free to flow.

I repeat, politicians grab the credit for what Creation has wrought. While no degree of temptation justifies any degree of sin, millions of politicians yield to temptation. Believing that they are the source of the bounties of our not-yet-destroyed freedom, they "think" that these gifts are theirs to dispense. Results of this gross ineptness? They become *predators*—"plundering or robbing." They indulge in legal thievery, having written the very statutes that make their actions legal!

Those who seek political power over others—those who would be human gods—are unaware how little they know. For God does not thus lord it over us. We are *free* to go His Way or not—to enjoy the rewards or suffer the penalties resulting from our actions.

Those of us who seek a society where everyone is free to act creatively as he or she pleases might well heed the wise counsel of one of the world's greatest statesmen, Edmund Burke:

Men are qualified for *civil liberty* in exact proportion to their disposition to put chains upon their own appetites; in proportion as their love of justice is above their rapacity; in proportion as their soundness and sobriety of understanding is above their vanity and presumption; in proportion as they are more disposed to listen to the counsels of the wise and good, in preference to the flattery of knaves. Society cannot exist unless a controlling power upon the will and appetite is placed somewhere; and the less of it there is within, the more there must be of it without. It is ordained in the eternal constitution of things, that men of intemperate habits cannot be free. Their passions forge their fetters.

If there is to be a return to freedom—and there will be—intemperate habits must be replaced with temperate habits. How do away with the passions that forge our fetters? Have the courage to say "*NO*" to all political chicanery: "political trickery."

It is ordained in the constitution of earthly life that freedom shall again bless our lives. Our role? *Yield not to temptation!*

# 17

# MAKING THE MOST OF ONE'S SELF

> *Whatever you are by nature, keep to it; never desert your own line of talent. Be what nature intended you for, and you will succeed; be anything else and you will be ten thousand times worse than nothing.*
>
> **—SYDNEY SMITH**

This English divine (1771–1845) recognized that, because all of us have different talents, doing what we should do leads to success. Right!

However, that last line of his befuddles me. What could be ten thousand times worse than nothing? This is exaggeration for the sake of emphasis, and it may blind us to another facet of truth. Wrote the American clergyman, Hosea Ballou (1771–1852): "Exaggeration is a blood relative of falsehood and nearly as blamable."

The eminent psychologist, Dr. Fritz Kunkel, offers a corrective and, in my opinion, voices a great truth: "*Immense hidden powers lurk in the unconscious of the most common man—indeed, of all people without exception.*"

We have in Dr. Kunkel's wisdom an excellent reason for never overlooking the potential that lies dormant in every human being. We find support for this openmindedness in Psalms 8:2: "Out of the mouths of babes and sucklings hast thou ordained strength."

"Strength" has ever so many meanings, ranging from brutal power over others to the courage of one's convictions. A few thoughts: "It is excellent to have a giant's strength," wrote Shakespeare, "but it is tyrannous to use it as a giant." Hitler and many politicians—in our country and elsewhere—exemplify this tyranny.

"Who is strong?" asked Benjamin Franklin. His answer: "He who conquers his bad habits."

What may we assume to be "strength" as used in Psalms? A strong aspiration—the strength to grow in awareness, perception, consciousness from babes evolving through all the decades of earthly life into mature adulthood. The lesson? For one's own sake, search for those who see through the darkness to light—seers!

The wisdom of Sydney Smith is confirmed by Emerson: "Nothing is rich but the inexhaustible wealth of nature. She shows us only the surfaces, but is million fathoms deep." Everything on earth or sea or sky is wondrous—from atoms to galaxies.

Reflect on the atom. It is so small that 30,000,000,000 could be placed on the period at the end of this sentence without overlapping. Blow up an atom to 100 yards in diameter and what does one behold? Radiant energy in the form of electrons in wave sequences flying about at the speed of light. In the center of the atom is the nucleus which, after the atom is expanded, is the size of a pinhead! This and this alone is "stuff" and no one knows what it is, except that it appears to be solid. All else is empty space. As everything in nature, all is mystery!

Were it possible to apply an atomic press to me and squeeze out all the "stuff"—the nuclei—I would be a particle so small that it would not be discernible on a piece of white paper. I am but a mere speck—next to nothing!

Galaxies? There are millions of them, constantly moving away from each other into the void of outer space. All in nature is mystery, including our infinitesimal know-how!

As to our infinitesimal know-how, Smith gave us good counsel: "never desert your own line of talent." Of all the people who have lived on this earth no two lines of talent have ever been identical, not even remotely.[1] Indeed, in each second of our earthly lives 1,000,000,000,000,000,000 atoms leave every human's body going every which way throughout the universe and a new quintillion replaces them.

As the famous chemist, Donald Hatch Andrews wrote: "And speaking very reverently, we can say that each of us has in his body a thousand atoms that were in the body of Christ . . . the individual atoms are scarcely more than the shadows of a far deeper reality that we find in this total atomic *harmony* within us, the spirit of our Creator within us."

Most citizens believe that a societal catastrophe would result if everyone were to act in his or her self-interest—creatively as each pleases. But not one of America's great economists, William Graham Sumner (1840–1910), who gave us this truth with its poetic

---

[1] See *You Are Extraordinary* by Roger J. Williams (New York: Pyramid Books, 1976).

conclusion: ". . . making the most of one's self . . . is not a separate thing from filling one's place in society, but *the two are one, and the latter is accomplished when the former is done.*"

A vast majority of people in this and other countries, including many noted scholars, confuse self-interest with selfishness. The definition of selfishness? ". . . having such regard for one's own interests and advantage that the happiness and welfare of others becomes of less concern than is considered right and just." Selfish individuals range all the way from thieves to political and private power mongers. All who gain at the expense of others fall in this despicable category!

Here are three fallacious observations by noted scholars.

Man seeks his own good at the whole world's cost.
                                                    *—Robert Browning*

Whom blood has joined together, self-interest jerks asunder.
                                                    *—La Fontaine*

The worst poison of an honest heart: self-interest.    *—Tacitus*

Confucius revealed the popular reaction toward those who pursue their self-interest. "He who works for his own interests arouses *much animosity.*"

John Stuart Mill, gifted with insight and foresight, was among the few to grasp the pursuit of self-interest as an efficacious way of life: "The only freedom which deserves the name is that of pursuing our own good *in our own way,* so long as we do not attempt to deprive others of theirs, or impede their efforts to obtain it."

The pursuit of self-interest as one's objective is more likely to be disparaged than applauded. Generally, acting in one's own interest is associated with greed, avarice, selfishness. This only demonstrates the extent of the confusion.

The truth? Self-interest is the motivator of creative human action. Minding one's own business amounts to serving oneself by serving others. This is a task of a size to fit the individual—whatever his talents. It can be one of life's *most fascinating and rewarding adventures*.

# 18

# RESOLUTION WORKS WONDERS

*You may be whatever you resolve to be. Determine to be something in the world, and you will be something. "I cannot," never accomplished anything. "I will try," has wrought wonders.* **—JOEL HAWES**

The American clergyman Hawes (1789–1867) further advised: "Aim at the sun, and you may not reach it; but your arrow will fly far higher than if aimed at an object on a level with yourself." Obviously, Hawes' "Aim at the sun" is symbolic of *the ideal,* namely, that which is perfect. An excellent commentary on this point comes from another American clergyman, Tryon Edwards (1809–94): "We never reach our ideals, whether of mental or moral improvement, but the thought of them shows us our deficiencies,. and spurs us on to higher and better things."

One need not be an atheist to behave as if there were nothing in the Cosmos above his or her own shoulders. Herds of citizens are completely unaware of why they live so well—on the fruits of the freedom socialism has not yet destroyed; they are not striving for mental and moral improvement. Such improvement might be stimulated by an idea I have recently encountered: whether realized or not, every moment is new and everything we think and do is new. *Creativity is constant!*

No person on this earth knows what happened—bad or good— during the last minute. Nor does anyone have the slightest idea about what will happen in the next minute. Whenever a person grasps the truth that *creativity is constant,* that individual is on the right road, *toward* the ideal. As Cervantes wrote, "The road is always better than the inn." Indeed, there is no inn, no stopping place on the way toward the ideal. The best one can do is to travel righteously every day of mortal life!

According to the French clergyman, René Almeron (1612–72): "The best and noblest lives are those who are set toward high ideals, and the highest and noblest ideal that any man can have is Jesus of Nazareth." No one could have a higher goal. While not attainable, 'tis a heavenly lodestar, an ideal toward which we should aim. The second coming of Jesus does not, in my view, mean another Jesus but, rather, personal striving to approximate His Holy Perfection!

How true that "I cannot" never accomplished anything. To apply it to every aspect of life would be to descend below the human level. But reflect on the millions who are afflicted to some degree with the "I cannot" syndrome—no thrust for higher levels, for growth in understanding. Wrote the English essayist, Sir Richard Steele (1672–1729): "I know of no evil so great as the abuse of understanding and yet there is no vice more common."

There are ever so many among my personal acquaintances who understand that the coercive prohibition of creative actions is evil.

One sample among thousands of creative actions will suffice: the freedom to exchange goods and services in this or any other country. They *understand* and, thus, believe that free trade is right. The performance? They *abuse their understanding* by failing to show the fallacy of embargoes, tariffs and other obstacles to free trade.

Why this abuse? The fear of criticism, the lack of courage to stand for what's right. In 1953 my FEE associate, Dr. W. M. Curtiss, wrote a booklet—*The Tariff Idea*—thoroughly exposing its flaws. It had two results: (1) an improved understanding by ever so many of this politico-economic fallacy and (2) a loss of many thousands of dollars in contributions to FEE. Had we known beforehand what these results would be, would we have presented our position to the 50,000 on our mailing list? An emphatic "*YES*"! Away with this common vice—fear of criticism!

Wrote the American author and editor, Christian N. Bovee (1820–1904): "There is great beauty in going through life without anxiety or fear. Half our fears are baseless, and the other half discreditable." Should seekers after the truth of freedom fear criticism? Never! Expect criticism from those espousing socialistic notions, but heed it no more than opposition from anyone in a position of special privilege that he wants to protect. Let such nonsense pass by as mere babble.

But what about criticism from those who seek to achieve a reasonable understanding and explanation of the freedom way of life? Heed them, indeed! Why? This is a fruitful way to discover one's own errors—the road to truth. Wrote Thomas Jefferson: "Error of opinion may be tolerated where reason is free to combat it."

Reason is "the power of comprehending . . . or thinking." Briefly, it is the power to advance in consciousness. It is possible that our third President derived this wisdom from the English poet,

John Milton (1608–74), who in 1644 wrote in *Areopagitica:* "Give me the liberty to know, to think, to believe, and to *utter freely,* according to *conscience,* above all other liberties."

Consciousness is *the* reality! One's aim in earthly life should be to advance in this respect as far as possible for the consciousness we succeed in attaining during our mortal moments is the consciousness that will belittle or bless us in the hereafter.

Why is the liberty to utter freely the most important of all liberties? There are at least two assurances that one is advancing mentally, morally and spiritually: (1) when he is working for the liberty of everyone to act creatively as he or she pleases and (2) when he is able proudly to present the truth of human liberty before The Source—Infinite Consciousness—and his compatriots.

Wrote Emerson: "A good intention clothes itself with power." Liberty has tremendous power for human advancement. *Resolve to work on its behalf!*

# 19

# THE GOOD WITHIN OUR REACH

*To improve the golden moment of opportunity and to catch the good that is within our reach, is the great art of life.* **—SAMUEL JOHNSON**

The English author and lexicographer, Samuel Johnson (1709–84) wrote the first English dictionary. His old home on Fleet Street remains as it was when he passed away and the original dictionary is on a stand that tourists may gaze at it. I have visited his place several times. Johnson was and still is one of the all-time greats.

Henry Ford the elder was an outstanding exemplar of Johnson's wisdom: "Coming together is a beginning, keeping together is progress, working together is success."

Suppose there were no coming together, each individual dependent solely on his or her own thoughts and productivity—no exchange of goods and services. All would starve! To prove this point, merely ask yourself, whoever you may be, how well you would prosper were you dependent on only that which you know how to do. The answer: no human togetherness, no humans—the

79

earth populated with lower forms of life, ranging from oysters to chimpanzees.

Why is coming together a beginning? Because it results in a pooling of our specializations. Americans are the most specialized people who ever existed. We have become interdependent; each of us is dependent on the unique specializations of others and *freedom to exchange*.

Upon what does freedom to exchange depend? On an honest medium of exchange—*money!* A viable exchange economy requires a money more substantial than irredeemable paper—a money that may not be depreciated at the whim of political leaders.

There is no question that *working together leads to success*. The problem is to maintain the freedom to cooperate and to compete. As the late Supreme Court Justice William O. Douglas remarked several years ago: "Today it is generally recognized that all corporations possess an element of public interest. A corporation director must think not only of the stockholder but also of the laborer, the supplier, the purchaser, and the ultimate consumer. Our economy is but a chain which can be no stronger than any one of its links. We all stand together or fall together in our highly industrialized society of today."

Ever since Justice Douglas wrote the above we have been falling ever deeper into a socialistic abyss. Why this dilemma? True, "corporations possess an element of public interest," a fact that is recognized by an enlightened few of the directors thereof, that is, they practice what they believe. Jolly well good, as the English say. But many compromise.

The exceptions to standing ramrod straight are, at this point in our history, appallingly numerous. The present situation is remindful of the ideological slump during the early days of the New Deal:

the National Industrial Recovery Act—the NRA or the Blue Eagle—became law.

Top business leaders and their national organizations endorsed this fantastic set of strangling controls over the economy. Indeed, it was a wealthy utility president who sold FDR on this scheme. Why this anti-free market position? For more reasons than I shall ever know but one was the hope of being rid of dreaded competition. However, after a year of this politico-economic nonsense, business leaders and their organizations reversed their position, but some dragged their feet. Abbreviated, their reasoning ran like this: "We must be rid of this political monstrosity, but let us eliminate it gradually. To get rid of it suddenly would wreck the economy."

Getting rid of what's wrong *gradually* is a nonsensical tactic, for gradualism has no end. Restore what's right *right now!* And that is what happened to NRA in May, 1935, with the Supreme Court's famous "Chicken Case" decision. As of that moment every phase of NRA was abolished, not an iota of it remained. The wrong abolished *suddenly!* Did the economy go smash? To the contrary, citizens went suddenly to work. Have a look at the indices—on the up! The opportunity of working together was increased.

Why did most businessmen fail to take advantage of this reborn opportunity? Justice Douglas points to the answer: "Our economy is but a chain which can be no stronger than any one of its links." What a brilliant analogy!

The failure of the Blue Eagle—for all its pitiful narrowing of opportunities—taught them not. Only a few learned the lesson and came to an understanding of how the free and unfettered market works its wonders for one and all!

Some time ago a noted professor of anthropology at a leading college condemned the market economy on the ground that cooperation was good, competition bad. What a fallacy! Example: When bakers of bread compete, the one who provides the best—highest quality at the lowest price—is the one with whom *we cooperate*. Competition and cooperation are twin virtues and when strictly observed they form what might well be called "The thank you society." When buying a loaf of bread for 75¢, I say "Thank you" because I want the bread more than the money. The grocer says "Thank you" because he wants the money more than the bread. This is the free market at the bread-and-butter level!

"To improve the golden moment of opportunity and to catch the good that is within our reach" requires numerous virtues, one of which is the *strict avoidance of compromise*. Wrote the American statesman, Charles Sumner (1811–74): "From the beginning of our history the country has been afflicted with compromise. It is by compromise that human rights have been abandoned. I insist that this shall cease. The country needs repose after all its trials; it deserves repose. And repose can only be found in everlasting principles."

Wrote Henry Ward Beecher: *"Expedients are for the hour; principles for the ages."*

# 20

# OUR WORK? TIME WILL TELL

*Not armies, not nations, have advanced the race; but here and there in the course of ages, an individual has stood up and cast his shadow over the world.*     **—E. H. CHAPIN**

This American clergyman (1814–80) was blest with hindsight and foresight. He knew of those sages over the centuries who stood foursquare for their righteous convictions, set examples for the advancing of the human race—cast their shadows over the world!

Some nations may have used their armies solely for defensive purposes, but most armies throughout world history have had only aggressive purposes. I feel personally involved in this matter, for my family has had quite a war record. My great-great-great-grand-father and my great-great-grandfather fought in the Revolutionary War, my grandfather in the Civil War, I in World War I, and my two sons in World War II. As I have written earlier, it has taken me all of these years to see the light.[1] I now see the nonsense of

---

[1]See the chapter, "War and Peace" in my book, *Awake for Freedom's Sake* (Irvington, N.Y.: The Foundation for Economic Education, Inc., 1977), pp. 30–39.

war; I see that the better alternative is free trade among nations. Dwight Eisenhower, with a far greater experience, had a view which I share: "When people speak to you about a preventive war, you tell them to go and fight it. After my experience, I have come to hate war. *War settles nothing!*"

A nation—apart from the families of men, women and children who comprise it—is a mere label for a piece of real estate. If the citizens are intelligent, industrious, honest and kind they make up a great nation regardless of the geography. This is just as true of the Union of Soviet Socialist Republics as of the United States of America. Apart from the people we have here only labels which mislead the thoughtless. Here are three among the many agreements with E. H. Chapin:

> Territory is but the body of a nation. The people who inhabit its hills and valleys are its souls, its spirit, its life.
>
> —*James A. Garfield*

> National progress is the sum of individual industry, energy and uprightness, as national decay is of individual idleness, selfishness and vice.          —*Samuel Smiles*

> The true grandeur of nations is in those qualities which constitute the true greatness of the individual.     —*Charles Sumner*

With reference to Samuel Smiles' observation, there is no need to elaborate on why national decay is born of individual idleness, selfishness and vice. The rise and fall of the Roman Empire is but one of many examples throughout all history. Paraphrasing the English poet, Lord Byron (1788–1824): "'Tis vice that digs her own voluptuous tomb."

Now for the opposite—the most remarkable demonstration of how "national progress is the sum of *individual* industry, energy and uprightness in all history." It took place in Florence when it was a nation and not a city as now. The Duke of Florence, known as Lorenzo the Magnificent (1449–92) was wealthy, a great scholar and had as much political power as any dictator who ever lived.

Lorenzo limited his great political power to keeping the peace. Florentians acted creatively as they pleased; an essentially free society prevailed which accounted for one of the greatest outbursts of creativity up to that time and laid the ground for the birth of the Italian Renaissance.

When Lorenzo passed on to his reward, his son, Piero, became the Duke whom the unlimited power corrupted. The Florentians drove that family—the Medici—out of their nation, never to return.[2] The rise for a good reason and a fall for an equally good reason!

Wrote Elisha Friedman: "When a national ideal dies, a nation perishes." Lorenzo's *ideal* died when his son, Piero, took over. The nation perished! I am reminded of a thought by Shakespeare: "Man, proud man! dressed in a little brief authority, plays such fantastic tricks before high heaven as make the angels weep."

The English poet, Samuel Butler, expressed the same idea a generation later in this enlightening jingle:

> Authority intoxicates,
> And makes mere sots of magistrates;
> The fumes of it invade the brain,
> And make men giddy, proud, and vain.

Lord Acton (1834–1902), added his wisdom: "Power tends to corrupt and absolute power corrupts absolutely." Here is the way my dictionary defines the kind of government that "makes the

---

[2]See *The Medici* by G. F. Young (New York: Modern Library).

angels weep,'' that "intoxicates,'' that "corrupts absolutely'': *"To
exercise authority over, direct; control; rule; manage."* Authoritarianism on the rampage!

In our America—once the home of the free—authoritarianism,
for the past few decades, has raged unchecked, increasing each
year by horrendous leaps toward a politico-economic hell. The
American theologian, Tryon Edwards (1809–94), cited the cause
of such a deplorable mess, of a kind that has infected the citizens
of all nations throughout history: "Hell is truth seen too late—
duty neglected in its season." And this wise man added: "Much
of the glory and sublimity of truth *is connected with its mystery.*
To understand everything we must be as God."

Duty's season is always past, present and future. Duty-vacations
are taboo! The late Robert A. Millikan, a FEE Trustee, one of the
world's greatest scientists and Nobel Prize winner in physics,
wrote: "Duty has nothing to do with what somebody else con-
ceives to be for the common good." Duty has to do with what you
and I conceive to be *for our own good.* What's for the common
good is a mystery to every citizen. Our one and only duty? Intellectual, moral and spiritual growth!

May our work—yours and ours—result in a return to freedom
for the U.S.A. and, hopefully, for the world. Let us be freemen
whom *the truth makes free!*

# 21

# THE TOUCHSTONE OF PROGRESS

*To have striven, to have made an effort, to have been true to certain ideals—this alone is worth the struggle.* **—SIR WILLIAM OSLER**

This Canadian physician (1849–1919) made another edifying and enlightening observation:

Though little, the master word looms large in meaning. It is the "open sesame" to every portal, the great equalizer, the philosopher's stone which transmutes all base metal of humanity into gold. The stupid it will make bright, the bright brilliant, and the brilliant steady. To youth it brings hope, to the middle-aged confidence, to the aged repose. It is directly responsible for all advances in medicine during the past 25 years. Not only has it been the touchstone of progress, but is the measure of success in everyday life. And the master word is *work!*

Another distinguished physician, Dr. Hans Selye, named several famous men who lived to a ripe old age, and added this comment: "Of course in their many years of intense activity, these people never "worked"; they lived a life of "leisure" by working at what they liked to do."[1] Here, at least in common terminology, is what appears to be a paradox in the lives of men of achievement: (1) "these people never worked" and (2) "they lived a life of leisure."

The individuals to whom Dr. Selye referred found occupations in harmony with their uniqueness. A labor of love! Hours? Long days and even nights! Years ago, FEE had a personal—not a government—garbage collector. Late one afternoon while he was emptying our garbage into his truck I asked, "How are you doing, Herbie?" He replied, "Mr. Read, I love my work."

Work, if of the kind one loves—be it Herbie's, yours or mine— is remindful of Thomas Edison's laughable but wise sentence: "As a cure for worrying, work is better than whiskey." Work, if joyous, is also a cure for fretting, despondency and doubt. The American surgeon, Dr. Charles A. Mayo (1865–1939), along with his brothers, established the Mayo Clinic in 1889. It gained international fame. Wrote this genius: "Worry affects the circulation, the heart, the glands, the whole nervous system. I have never known a man who died from overwork, but many who died from doubt."

True, many die from doubt, defeated by years of hopelessness, having no goals to encourage life's advancement. "Doubt is brother devil to despair." It is clear that we should steer clear of doubt. How? Have faith in intellectual, moral and spiritual growth. "Faith is the subtle chain that binds us to the Infinite."

Conceded, the touchstone of progress is in working at the joyous

---

[1] See a splendid article, "But Hard Work Isn't Bad for You," by Dr. Hans Selye, *Reader's Digest*, June, 1973.

level—each person in harmony with his or her uniqueness. It seems appropriate here to quote and comment on what several among the thoughtful have had to say about progress.

All that is human must retrograde if we do not advance.
—*Edward Gibbon*

There is no staying in one position—except under a tombstone. Alive, we change one way or the other every second. "We shall all be changed in a moment, in the twinkling of an eye." (I Corinthians, 15:51–52)

He that is good will infallibly become better, and he that is bad, will as certainly become worse; for vice, virtue and time are three that never stand still.        —*Caleb C. Colton*

Every moment of life should be aimed at surpassing the previous moment. Look not only to self but to the sages, past and present. If one's goal be the advancement of liberty, study the works of Confucius, Socrates, Emerson, Bastiat, our Founding Fathers and ever so many others including the works of the late Benjamin Rogge. Not to advance in good thinking is to fall by the wayside. Lacking a worthy purpose, life drifts downhill; to mount higher demands effort.

Every age has its problems by solving which, humanity is helped forward.        —*H. Heine*

We Americans have been experiencing a problem growing worse during each decade since 1898: SOCIALISM! Humanity is helped forward only if and when freedom—civilization—has prevailed, and these instances are few in number.

The first eruption of truth—a move toward freedom—took place in Sumer, now known as Iraq, 4,600 years ago. About a century ago, some archeologists began excavating in that arid and non-productive land. They went deeper than originally intended, coming upon fantastic surprises: beautiful buildings, artistic sculptures and other works of art and, above all, clay tablets, prisms and cones by the thousands, all done in cuneiform signs, setting forth the freedom philosophy, religion, and so on.[2] While this, as the ones that follow, cannot be described as a state of perfection, each was attended by a prosperity previously unknown.

The second eruption occurred in ancient Athens, described by Edith Hamilton. ". . . the shadow of 'effortless barbarism' was dark upon the face of the earth. In that black and fierce world a little centre of white-hot spiritual energy was at work. A new civilization had arisen in Athens, unlike all that had gone before."

Admittedly, it was not like ancient Sumer, but Athens was featured by an unparalleled freedom for that day and age. And Athens flourished for a time.

For the third eruption of truth, move on to medieval times: Venice in the heyday of Marco Polo (1250–1325). In this instance there was freedom to produce and exchange with others thousands of miles away. Again, unprecedented wealth! Exceptional? Observe Venice today! In the same all-too-common mess again.

For the fourth eruption of truth refer to Adam Smith and one of the greatest books ever written: *The Wealth of Nations*. It was his book and the help of John Bright, Richard Cobden and Frederic Bastiat that resulted in the overthrow of mercantilism—the thing we now call the planned economy or welfare state. Result? The Industrial Revolution, the greatest boon to the masses up until that

---

[2]For detailed information see two books by Samuel Noah Kramer: *From the Tablets of Sumer* (Indian Hills, Colorado: The Falcon's Press), 1956, and *The Sumerians: Their History, Culture and Character* (Chicago: The University of Chicago Press), 1963.

time. But, again the slump, back to the same old mess again. Recently, a hoped-for political turnabout. Maybe yes and maybe no!

And finally the greatest eruption of all time: the U.S.A.—for a time! And do not overlook the role of Adam Smith as related to the American miracle. It was the simultaneous appearance of *The Wealth of Nations* and the Declaration of Independence, followed by the Constitution and the Bill of Rights, that put government in its proper place and left Americans free to act creatively as they pleased. The result? By far the greatest flourishing of creative energy ever known, and a prosperity beyond the dreams of all who had gone before.

The U.S.A. another example of the rise and fall sequence? Yes, we are witnessing the same kind of fall that England experienced—except that our fall is from a higher level. The reason why we are still so prosperous is the enormous momentum from the time when we were freer than today. The ways of freedom are still in our blood, and they continue to serve even when not understood. Thank Heaven, we still have time to bring about a reversal.

As to the touchstone of progress, I shall conclude by quoting the American author and editor, Christian N. Bovee (1820–1904): "The greatest of all laws is the law of progressive development. Under it, men grow wiser as they grow older."

One does not grow old; one becomes old by not growing. As we grow older, let us grow wiser in understanding and explaining the birth of the American miracle: *freedom to act creatively as we please!*

# 22

# ALL IS MYSTERY

*Mystery is but another name for ig-
norance; if we were omniscient, all
would be perfectly plain.*
**—TRYON EDWARDS**

The wise Tryon Edwards (1809–94) presents a thought which, if grasped and adhered to, would be a boon to mankind.

First, what is the meaning of omniscient? It is: "Infinite knowledge; knowing all things." Perhaps there is no greater thwarting of human evolution than the millions of know-it-alls who "think" of themselves as omniscient—as God—whereas they are about as far from such Enlightenment as humans can get. To them, very little, if anything, is mystery!

Second, what is mystery? It is: "Something unexplained, unknown, or kept secret; as *the mystery of life*." It is, indeed, another name for the ignorance which is part of our finitude.

Everything in life is mystery—*no exception* whatsoever! Begin by asking a relevant question, "How can I have my way and at the same time do no injury or injustice to others?"

Perhaps the answer will come clear if I can find the answer to two other questions, (1) Who am I? and (2) Where am I going? or, better yet, What is my way? Another phrasing of these questions might be: (1) What is man's nature? and (2) What is man's destiny? These speculations are as ancient as man himself. Although they are beyond the capacity of any person to answer, some light may be shed as one wrestles with them.

Who am I? Here's one part of the answer: I am one octillion atoms — 1,000,000,000,000,000,000,000,000,000 — a number difficult to grasp unless we use our imagination. Cover the surface of this earth—land and sea—with dried peas to a depth of four feet and their number would fall far, far short of an octillion. Go out into the universe and cover 250,000 other earth-sized planets with four feet of peas and that would be the number of atoms in my make-up.[1] Mystery?

The atom? It is so small that 30 trillion atoms could be placed on the period at the end of this sentence without overlapping. Blow an atom up to 100 yards in diameter and what do you behold? Radiant energy in the form of electrons, neutrons and the like, in wave sequences flying about at the speed of light. In the center is the atomic nucleus which, after being thus expanded, is the size of a pinhead. This and this alone is "stuff" and no one knows what it is, except that it appears "solid." All else is empty space. Mystery?

Were it possible to apply an atomic press to me and squeeze out all but the "stuff"—the nuclei—I would be a particle so small that it would not be discernible on a piece of white paper. In a word, I am physically but a mere speck—next to nothing! Mystery?

---

[1]See "The New Science and The New Faith" by Donald Hatch Andrews, *The Freeman*, April 1961.

As for the other side of the coin, there is a sense in which I am even more than a mere, mechanistic speck—infinitely more. For instance, my octillion atoms are not the same atoms that comprised my make-up a few years ago. They continuously escape and a new octillion enters about every five years. To where do they escape and from whence come the new ones? To and from everywhere throughout the universe! As the famous scientist, Dr. Andrews, wrote: "There is a high probability that you have in your body right now a thousand atoms that were once in the body of Julius Caesar . . . and speaking very reverently, we can say that each of us has in his body a thousand atoms that were in the body of Christ . . . the individual atoms are scarcely more than the shadows of a far deeper reality that we find in this total atomic *harmony* within us, the spirit of our Creator within us."

Wrote the Swiss theologian, John Lavater (1741–1801): "Each particle of matter is an immensity; each leaf a world; each insect an inexplicable compendium."

Charles F. Kettering, famous engineer and inventor (1876–1958) said, "No one knows why grass is green."

Here is a supporting stunner. Two acres of our lawn at FEE have over one billion blades of grass and this is an infinitesimal fraction of all the grass on earth—each blade "a world," that is, a *mystery!*

After retiring, I often look through my bedroom window and observe headlights of autos some distance away. The source of these lights, countless millions of them in many countries? Electricity! Not a soul on earth knows *what* it is, only *that* it is and a few clues as to what it can do!

Every breath, all heartbeats, eyesight, the billions of cells in the human cortex, the ability to wonder, the evolution of humanity—blessings without end—are mysteries!

Wrote F. D. Huntington (1819–1904): "While reason is puzzling herself about the mystery, *faith* is turning it into daily bread and feeding on it thankfully in our heart of hearts." Heart of hearts?: "in one's innermost nature or deepest feelings; fundamentally."

"Miracle is the darling child of faith." And so is mystery for the right-minded. Mystery, if and when recognized—an awareness of how little we know—makes the case for liberty: for it is a mysterious fact that our tiny bits of expertise, freely flowing, become the goods and services by which we live and prosper.

Wrote the American clergyman, Robert Collyer (1823–1912): "Faith makes the discords of the present, the harmonies of the future." Recognize that mystery is everywhere, and *have faith in liberty for one and all!*

# 23

# THE STEPPINGSTONES TO KNOWLEDGE

> *It was said of one of the most intelligent men who ever lived in New England, that when asked how he came to know so much about everything, he replied, "By constantly realizing my own ignorance, and never being afraid or ashamed to ask questions."*  **—TRYON EDWARDS**

In his compilation of *The New Dictionary of Thoughts*, the American theologian, Tryon Edwards (1809–94) found others to confirm his views:

> The first step to knowledge is to know that we are ignorant.
> *—Richard Cecil*

> By ignorance is pride increased; those most assume who know the least.  *—John Gay*

Ignorance deprives men of freedom because they do not know what alternatives there are. It is impossible to choose to do what one has never "heard of."                    —*Ralph Barton Perry*

Anyone with a modicum of wisdom realizes the absurdity of running the lives of others. No one knows perfectly how to run his or her own life. It is said that "Pride goeth before a fall." The millions overly proud account for the fall that *has been* upsetting the freedom way of life.

I use the past tense, "has been," because of a firm belief that the societal pendulum has swung to the left—toward socialism—as far as it is going to go, and that it is about to swing toward the right—the freedom way of life. To be found in Matthew 5:38–39: "Ye have heard that it hath been said, An eye for an eye, and a tooth for a tooth. I say unto you. That ye resist not evil; but whosoever shall smite thee on the *right* cheek, turn to him the other [*left*] also."

Here we have the use of "right" and "left" about 2,000 years ago. The counsel is of the highest order, namely, effective resistance to socialistic know-it-all-ness does not consist in smiting them—name-calling and so on—but only by the positive approach: presenting the case for liberty far better than we have been doing. Admittedly, the turnabout will be a miracle but as Goethe said, "Miracle is the darling child of faith." We must have faith to win!

I have written time and time again that faith works miracles. Here are several proofs that I am an ideological and a politico-economic copycat and proud of it—looking for wisdom from my superiors:

There is no great future for any people whose faith has burned out or congealed. History records the ominous fact that national degeneration takes place where faith or vision fail or wane as

surely as it does when economic assets shrink or when there is
a dearth of sound money currency.            —*Rufus M. Jones*

Faith marches at the head of the army of progress. It is found
beside the most refined life, the freest government, the profoundest philosophy, the noblest poetry, the purest humanity.
                                              —*T. T. Munger*

Never yet did there exist a full faith in the divine word which
did not expand the intellect while it purified the heart; which did
not multiply the aims and objects of the understanding, while it
fixed and simplified those of the desires and passions.

                                              —*Coleridge*

We are establishing an all-time world record in the production
of material things. What we lack is a righteous and dynamic
faith. Without it, all else avails us little. The lack cannot be
compensated for by politicians, however able; or by diplomats,
however astute; or by scientists, however inventive; or by bombs,
however powerful.                         —*John Foster Dulles*

We, members of society, can expect no beneficial results short
of a faith in—and practice of—righteousness, the Golden Rule
being an excellent guideline: Never do unto others that which you
would not have them do unto you. Dulles rejects bombs, however
powerful; which is to say that mass murder multiplies rather than
lessens mankind's problems. I have recently written a pamphlet,
*Conscience on the Battlefield,* an attempt on my part to demonstrate the absurdity of such action.[1]

Enough about the ignorance that torments all who have lived or
now live. Let us reflect on its opposite, knowledge, that we may
find the right steppingstones and move toward the proper goals;

---

[1] Copy on request.

for "Knowledge advances by *steps,* not by leaps," as Macaulay reminds us. Daniel Webster added his wisdom: "Knowledge is the only fountain, both of the love and the principles of human liberty."

We have American history to prove this point. Our Founding Fathers were knowledgeable—statesmen, not politicians. In their search for righteousness they unseated government as the endower of men's rights and placed the Creator there. George Washington phrased it excellently: "If to please the people, we offer what we ourselves disapprove, how can we afterwards defend our work? Let us raise a standard to which the wise and honest can repair. The event is in the hand of God."

Wrote Emerson: "Our knowledge is the amassed thought and experience of innumerable minds." Suppose that you or I knew no more than that which is or has been original with us. Each of us would be a dummy or, to use the German term, a "dummkopf." Socrates referred to himself as "a philosophical midwife." He received from countless sources and shared. Those of us who have a modicum of knowledge do the same. The Sage of Concord has been and still is one of the innumerable minds I draw upon.

No one is expert in all subjects, so let us emphasize in our writing and conversation whatever our unique knowledge happens to be. The more we practice what we know, the more skilled we become, and our improved bits of wisdom should be employed on the next occasion, and the next. Put the best foot forward, as the saying goes.

Doing what is right and proper, such as adhering to the Ten Commandments and The Golden Rule, are gifts of Creation. Knowledge at your and my level is awareness of how the free and unfettered market works its wonders. When tiny bits of expertise—there are trillions of them—are free to flow, they configurate and result in ever-improving lives and livelihood. Let's be worthy of our Heavenly gifts that others may build on what we have begun.

Finally, let us heed the counsel of the English educator, Thomas Arnold (1795–1842): "Real knowledge, like everything else of value, is not to be obtained easily. It must be worked for, studied for, thought for, and more than all, must be prayed for." *Let us pray for a knowledge of freedom!*

# 24

# WHAT THE LOOKING GLASS REVEALS

*Do you know the man against whom you have most reason to guard yourself? Your looking glass will give you a very fair likeness of his face.*
**—RICHARD WHATELY**

Among the highest virtues of mankind is self-control and the Archbishop of Dublin (1787–1863) clearly identified the individual in charge: Yours Truly!

Wrote Goethe, "What is the best government? That which teaches us to govern ourselves." The lesson? Those of us who would achieve self-mastery have only one guideline: strive for an understanding and explanation of Creation at the human level. This is an aspiration that can only be approximated, never achieved, no matter how brilliant one may be. Wrote the Spanish poet, dramatist and novelist, Miguel de Cervantes (1547–1616), "The road is always better than the inn." If we truly seek freedom, founded on self-control, then there is no inn, no graduating class, so long as life endures. It is always the road—refinement and more refinement—now and forever. And fear not repetition, for nothing is too often repeated that is not sufficiently learned. Repetition is the mother of learning!

Several excellent thoughts by the American divine, Wilbur Fisk (1792–1839): "Every temptation that is resisted, every noble aspiration that is encouraged, every sinful thought that is repressed, every bitter word that is withheld, adds its little item to the impetus of that great movement which is bearing upward toward a richer life and higher character."

Regardless of how great the temptation, it justifies no degree of sin, that is, no departure from truth as one beholds it. "The truth shall make you free!"

Edmund Burke came to our aid: "Nobility is a graceful ornament to the civil order. It is the Corinthian capital of polished society. It is, indeed, one sign of a liberal and benevolent mind to incline to it with some sort of partial propensity." Propensity? It means learning, readiness and the like—intellectually moving in the right direction, an aim all of us should have!

As to nobility, it is, indeed, the graceful ornament to civil— stately—order. Emerson: "All nobility in its beginnings, was somebody's natural superiority." In this sense, our Founding Fathers were *NOBLEMEN!* Why? They unseated government as the endower of human rights and placed the Creator there! I, and everyone, should salute them!

Enough about Fisk's noble aspirations. What about "every temptation that is resisted"? It is one thing to be tempted by monstrous and evil schemes such as socialism or any coercive device, but it is intellectual folly or sin to yield.

Observed the English critic and essayist, John Ruskin (1819– 1900): "No one can ask honestly or hope fully to be delivered from temptation unless he has himself honestly and firmly determined to do the best he can to keep out of it." In Matthew 6:13: "Lead us not into temptation but deliver us from evil."

Every sinful thought that is repressed increases the good thoughts that are within one's potentialities. The recognition of sin is the beginning of moral and politico-economic salvation. Wrote the founder of Pennsylvania, William Penn: "If thou wouldst conquer thy weakness thou must never gratify it. No man is compelled to evil; only his consent makes it his. It is no sin to be tempted; it is to yield and be overcome."

Perhaps an individual's greatest weakness is when he fancies himself wise. All populations are infested with know-it-alls. Pretended omniscience is a self-imposed liability, not coercively inflicted by others. All of us are tempted, but a few, bless their souls, do not succumb. They lead the rest of us in the righteous way.

Every bitter word that is withheld is a blessing in disguise. Regardless of the derogatory names communists or other masters of coercion may call those of us who are freedom devotees, let us refrain from biting back. When one calls another a "so-and-so," he reveals his own character. If one is improving, he doesn't wholly agree with his self of yesterday. Bear in mind that the *evolutionary thrust*—Creation's design for mankind—is toward an ever-expanding variation. Is it not obvious that bitter words, written or spoken to those who differ, hardens them in their ways? Instead of grasping any worthy ideas offered, they will turn their backs and assess the name-callers. "Thou fool!" It is tolerance and kindness that work wonders.

Wilbur Fisk's wisdom, concerning character, is confirmed by Samuel Smiles: "Good character is human nature in its best form. It is moral order embodied in the individual. Men of character are not only the conscience of society, but in every well-governed state they are its best motive power; for it is moral qualities which, in the main, rule the world.''

No question about it, character is human nature in its best form. It is the know-how and the determination to become an attracting exemplar of liberty for one and all. Such good thoughts, if their progenitors be numerous enough, do, indeed, rule the world!

Wrote the Sage of Concord: "A man passes for what he is worth. What he is engraves itself on his face in letters of light.'' To whom should one look for an ever-brighter light—understanding—of liberty? At *the face seen in the looking glass!*

## 25

# ONE WAY TO ASSESS THE FUTURE

*Tell me what are the prevailing sentiments that occupy the minds of your young men and I will tell you what is to be the character of the next generation.*
**—EDMUND BURKE**

Edmund Burke was a statesman, not a politician. He was one of the outstanding spokesmen and exponents of liberty. Burke, more than anyone else, opposed the Crown in its behavior toward the Colonies. Were Burke a present-day American, we would invite him to be a member of FEE's Board. I say this because I quote him more than any person past or present.

I have argued for years that prognostication—trying to predict the future—is nonsense. We have ever so many high IQers who are prophets of doom. They see the devolution of the past eight decades and conclude that that is IT! Such "prophets" are blind to the fact that evolution inevitably follows devolution. We have all history to demonstrate that this is part and parcel of the Cosmic Design. Actually, no one knows what is going to happen in the next minute.

We must not, however, overlook the fact that there is a rule of life which seems like prognostication, but is something quite different. It is an acknowledgment of the workings of cause and effect in human affairs; we reap what we have sown. Wrote Samuel Johnson, author of the first English dictionary, "The first years of men must make provision for the last." This squares with Burke's wisdom.

The above suggests that the future of our country rests on what present-day children will be like when advancing into adulthood and old age. Two samples of the very few who saw the light as did Burke and Johnson:

Childhood shows the man, as morning shows the day.

*—John Milton*

The child is father of the man.          *—William Wordsworth*

What is the "problem" we face? Appropriate education of our youngsters! Education falls into two opposite categories: (1) coercive, be it private or public; and (2) voluntary, with three major points which I shall attempt to explain.

Here are the two opposite philosophies, the first by that famous dictator, Napoleon: "Public instruction should be the first object of government." He, more than anyone, was responsible for government "education" in the U.S.A.[1]

Here is the second, the opposite of the dictator's nonsense and by a young lad, Andrew Carnegie, born in Scotland who had

---

[1]For an explanation see the chapter, "Elementary Education" in my book, *Liberty: Legacy of Truth* (Irvington, N.Y.: The Foundation for Economic Education, Inc., 1978), pp. 98–103.

hardly any formal schooling: "Look out for the boy who has to plunge into work direct from the common school and who begins by sweeping out the office. He is probably the dark horse you had better watch." Hard work was Carnegie's schooling. Did it succeed? This man founded the Carnegie Steel Company, the world's largest at the time, and became one of the world's wealthiest men and philanthropists.

What are the three major points we should understand and have the ability to explain? They are: (1) the locus of responsibility for the child's education; (2) the fallacy of government education; and (3) the efficacy of private education when understood and properly directed.

The responsibility for the education of children rests with the parents. For how long? Until the child matures into self-responsibility. If never, the problem is not educational but custodial. In brief, avoid present trends in "education." Wrote Tryon Edwards: "Sin with the multitude, and your responsibility and guilt are as great and as truly personal as if you alone had done the wrong."

Parents may hire a tutor as an educational aide. The right to hire has its counterpart: the right to fire. Bear in mind that authority and responsibility are commensurate. They are twin behaviors in all successful organization.

The second part is intended as a critique of government education, not as a criticism of all who teach in government schools, many of whom are committed to freedom. How do we know this? Over the past 35 years we have had many hundreds of teachers at FEE Seminars, and they are teaching the private ownership, free market, limited government way of life—liberty for one and all. Shall FEE take the credit? No, for our efforts would have been futile had we not been working with the *seekers of Truth!*

The three characteristics of government education? They are:

(1) Compulsory attendance.
(2) Government prescribed curricula.
(3) Forcible collection of the wherewithal to defray costs.

Compulsion is freedom's most antagonistic behavior! Instruction cannot be forced into another's head. Good ideas are to be attained by freely searching for the thoughts of superior mentors, past and present.

As to government-prescribed curricula: this is indoctrination, not education, and presupposes that those in political office think of themselves as know-it-alls. Wrote the English divine, Robert South: "Nothing is so haughty and assuming as ignorance where self-conceit sets up to be infallible."

The English poet and satirist, Samuel Butler, phrased this nonsense better:

> Authority intoxicates,
> And makes sots of magistrates;
> The fumes of it invade the brain,
> And make men giddy, proud, and vain.

The forcible collection of the wherewithal to pay for government education compels freedom devotees to subsidize their opponents.

My conclusion is intended to suggest free market education as the appropriate alternative to government education.

Government is organized police force; its appropriate and limited function is to keep the peace and invoke a common justice. Were government to step aside in education, as it has in religion, education would be left to the free market where the wisdom is.

Would the elimination of government from education mean that children would go unschooled? Not at all! Time after time I have asked individuals, from taxi drivers to corporate presidents, "Would you let your children go uneducated were all government compulsions removed?" Answer: "Do you think I am a fool? I would no more let my children go without an education than let them go without food."

The belief in freedom in education is in the form of an achievement in understanding (1) the nature of government, (2) its uniqueness as police force, and (3) the limited competence of, as well as the absolute necessity for, police force—an understanding to be learned, mastered, and remembered by at least enough persons to form an effective leadership in each new generation. This achievement is a personal, day-in and day-out requirement, meaning that it cannot be delegated to others, much less to our forefathers; it can never be relegated to the past tense; it is a *continuing* imperative of each new moment, without end.

The dilemma is this: The understanding of police-force-as-guard will, obviously, never be advanced but only retarded when the police-force-as-boss is put in the educational driver's seat. Thus, unless a breakthrough is achieved by an individual here and there, capable of independent analysis and unafraid of parting company with the masses, the most important aspect of education for responsible citizenship will go unattended.

The myth of government education, in our country today, is an article of general faith. To question the myth is to tamper with the faith, a business that few will read about or listen to or calmly tolerate. In short, for those who would make the case for educational freedom as they would for freedom in religion, let them be warned that this is a first-rate obstacle course. But heart can be taken in the fact that the art of becoming is composed of acts of overcoming. And becoming is life's prime purpose; becoming is, in fact, enlightenment—self-education *its own reward!*

## 26

# HAVE A STRONG CLEAR PURPOSE

*There is no road to success but through a strong clear purpose. Nothing can take its place. A purpose underlies character, culture, position, advancement of every sort.*
**—T. T. MUNGER**

Purpose is defined as "something one intends to get or do; intention, aim." Munger, an American clergyman (1830–1910), emphasized that the road to success, in any field, is paved with high aims. Tryon Edwards contributed a supporting thought: "High aims form high characters, and great objects bring out great minds." We should, for our own good, be able to identify those among us who possess a clear strong purpose. This can be aided—made easier—by reflecting on those poor souls who are afflicted with low—hellish—aims or purposes.

Wrote James Russell Lowell: "Not failure but low aim is crime."

In all of my 27 books I have emphasized time and time again that, in the politico-economic realm, none have a lower aim than those who seek coercive power in order to cast others in their pitiful, little images. Know-it-alls!

So, to avoid unncessary repetition, I shall quote what others have had to say about low ambitions.

The man who . . . seeks all things, wherever he goes, reaps from the hopes which he sows, a harvest of barren regrets.
*—Bulwer-Lytton*

Fling away ambition. By that sin angels fell. How then can man, the image of his Maker, hope to win by it?     *—Shakespeare*

Ambition often puts men upon doing the meanest offices. So climbing is performed in the same posture as creeping.
*—Jonathan Swift*

Ambition is a lust that is never quenched but grows more in-flamed and madder by enjoyment.     *—Thomas Otway*

Striving for fame and popularity fall into this same ignoble category.

Munger's "road to success" is consistent with the dictionary's definition of success: "a *favorable* or satisfactory outcome, or result." But success has its risks. Ever so many wise men have assessed individual success as having a pitiful effect—fat-headed-ness—the I-am-it syndrome. "Nothing fails like success," wrote Dean Inge; and Benjamin Franklin observed that "Success has ruined many a man." And it has!

Franklin, on another occasion, used a clever aphorism, some-what of an aboutface: "Success after forty is working for it like sixty." Many an individual, after achieving success during the vigorous years, is inclined to rest on his or her laurels. This is to fall by the wayside, to call it quits, to think of life's mission as already accomplished—creative action in the past tense. One must avoid such catastrophic nonsense and regard youthful success merely as the foundation for improvement—growth—in all of life's tomorrows.

When we discover that each individual is unique—not remotely like any other—each person being the best judge of the field in which his growth is most promising, we will all do our best to see that freedom of choice is maximized—liberty for one and all!

Wrote Albert Einstein: "A successful man is he who receives a great deal from his fellowmen, usually incomparably more than corresponds to his service to them." What a truism by this great scientist! According to this definition, I am a successful man, for I work to advance a cause which I believe is uppermost among mankind's countless goals—trying better to understand and explain the freedom way of life.

Do I receive incomparably more from others than they from me? Trillions of times more! From whence comes the pen with which I write? Not from any one person but from the tens of thousands who had a tiny part in its making. Reflect on the countless individuals who had a part in the food you and I eat, the clothes we wear, the cars we drive, the planes on which we travel, our telephones which can send our voices around the world in one-seventh of a second! I, as any other person, cannot even scratch the surface in recognizing our incomparable blessings!

Were enough persons aware of Einstein's truth, liberty would prevail. Why this assertion? They would reject any and all obstacles to the free flow of the trillions times trillions of blessings that account for our existence.

Andrew Carnegie, founder of United States Steel and one of America's greatest entrepreneurs and philanthropists—only nine months of schooling—wrote: "I believe the true road to prominent success in any line is to make yourself *master of that line*." Carnegie practiced what he preached, a laudable virtue—constancy of purpose! Thomas Carlyle wrote: "A man without a purpose is like a ship without a rudder—a waif, a nothing, a no man. Have a purpose in life, and having it, throw such strength of mind and muscle into your work as God [Creation] has given you."

To conclude, no one ever knows for certain who first spoke or wrote helpful truths. Here is one generally attributed to Emerson and also claimed by Elbert Hubbard: "If a man can write a better book, preach a better sermon or make a better mouse-trap than his neighbors, though he build his home in the woods, the world will make a beaten path to his door." "The world," as here used, is a metaphor, meaning unusually large numbers, not everyone on earth.

As to a better book, millions beat a path to those who wrote the *Holy Bible*. Reflect on the numbers who over the decades beat a path to Adam Smith's *Wealth of Nations,* and who have beaten and still are beating a path to Weaver's *The Mainspring of Human Progress,* Bastiat's *The Law* and ever so many others.

Sermons? How about "The Sermon on the Mount"? And the millions who are attracted to the moral and spiritual Perfection of Jesus? The law of attraction at its best!

Or build a better mouse-trap? Again, a metaphor! Individuals exercising their unique capabilities to achieve their full potential.

Let us try everlastingly to move ahead on the road to success. The guideline? *If at first you don't succeed try and try again!*

## 27

# STRIVE TO BE A NOBLEMAN

*True nobility is derived from virtue,
not from birth. Title may be purchased, but virtue is the only coin
that makes the bargain valid.*
**—RICHARD E. BURTON**

What a noble observation by this American author and professor of English (1861–1940)! "Nobleman," in its generic sense, is a man or woman inheriting at birth such titles as King, Lord, Prince, Duke, or a woman having the rank of "peer in her own right."

However, not all such labels are inheritances. I have an elderly friend on whom the title of "Lord" was recently bestowed. Why? Because of his virtue! These exceptions, throughout history, are numerous. I know of a Prince who is a freedom devotee.

My comments in no way contradict the accuracy of Burton's truisms. Error is too often mistaken for truth, for error is all about us and truth lies deep and must be searched for. As Austin O'Malley phrased this point: Truth lives in the cellar, error on the doorstep.

What about "title may be purchased"? Many titles, throughout recorded time, have been "purchased" by brute force. To name several examples: Napoleon, Mussolini, Hitler, Mao Tse-tung, Stalin.

What, really, is brute force? Is this a tyranny only of the past, a vice to be forgotten? Perish such a thoughtless notion!

A bum with a gun who robs another of his or her possessions obviously resorts to brute force. Even this kind of a low-brow bum wouldn't disagree! It's when a significant percentage of the citizenry descends to the Napoleonic level that titles are "purchased" by brute force.

Those who descend to this infamous level fall into two categories: (1) the millions of politicians who rob Peter to pay Paul and (2) the millions of Pauls who encourage and vote for the political robbers.

Is brute force implicit in this ignoble procedure? Yes, or the whole kit and caboodle of interventions by our 78,000 governments—federal, state and local—could be spoken of in the past tense.

These interventions are by the countless thousands. Several examples: social security, many forms of welfarism, government mail "delivery," coercive labor union tactics, embargoes, tariffs, government "education," local swimming pools, other special privileges in every town, city and state in the nation, the Gateway Arch being typical.

Are these interventions backed by brute force? Affirmative! For proof, try breaking these laws. Result? A fine or jail! Freedom of choice down the political drain! Napoleonic? Yes, indeed! Let us strive for their Waterloo!

Here is a suggestion as to the kind of thinking that, hopefully, might bring about a "Waterloo" to the employers of brute force—

unrestrained and devilish action: It is incorrect to think of liberty as synonymous with unrestrained action. Liberty does not and cannot include any action, regardless of sponsorship, which lessens the liberty of a single human being. To argue contrarily is to claim that liberty can be composed of liberty negations, patently absurd. Unrestraint carried to the point of impairing the liberty of others is the exercise of license, not liberty. To minimize the exercise of license is to maximize the area of liberty. Ideally, government would restrain license, not indulge in it; make it difficult, not easy; disgraceful, not popular. A government that does otherwise is licentious, not liberal.[1]

*True nobility is derived from virtue.* The English clergyman, Caleb Colton, expressed this point with clarity: "There is but one pursuit in life which it is in the power of all to follow, and of all to attain. It is subject to no disappointments, since he that perseveres makes every difficulty an advancement, and every conquest a victory; and this is the pursuit of virtue. Sincerely to aspire after virtue is to gain her; and zealously to labor after her ways is to receive them."

Virtue? According to my dictionary it is "Manliness . . . general moral excellence; right action and thinking; goodness of character." What a boon to mankind were a few as perfect as this definition suggests. However, no individual is or ever has been anywhere near perfect—Godlike! But bear in mind that there is no better aspiration, an ideal to be sought constantly, never forsaken. This truth inspired the English divine, A. W. Hare (1792–1884) to write: "They who disbelieve in virtue because man *has never been found perfect,* might as reasonably deny the sun because it is not always noon." Believe in virtue!

---

[1] I have used "liberal" in its classical sense. As my dictionary records: . . . originally, suitable for a freeman; not restricted; now obsolete.

Wrote the French archbishop, Francis Fenelon (1651–1715): "The most virtuous of all men, says Plato, is he who contents himself with being virtuous without seeking to appear so."

Seeking to appear virtuous is the pursuit of fame, an infamous goal.

For what is understood by *Fame*
Beside the getting of a *Name?*                     —*Swift*


Fame is nothing but an empty name.        —Charles Churchill


So let us content ourselves *by being virtuous!*

# NAME INDEX